The
Preaching Event

The
Preaching
Event

WILLIAM L. MALCOMSON

THE WESTMINSTER PRESS
Philadelphia

LIBRARY OF CONGRESS CATALOG CARD No. 68–23449

BOOK DESIGN BY
DOROTHY ALDEN SMITH

Published by The Westminster Press ®
Philadelphia, Pennsylvania

PRINTED IN THE UNITED STATES OF AMERICA

THIS BOOK IS DEDICATED TO
LAURIE, WARREN, AND ROBERT
WHO HAVE ENCOURAGED ME

Contents

Introduction

THIS IS A BOOK ABOUT PREACHING. It begins with a rationale for preaching. Most books on preaching begin this way. The next section deals with the congregation. My reason for discussing the congregation at this point in the book is that preaching is always directed *to* people. It is not something the preacher does for himself or by himself. Ideally, it is a joint venture of preacher and congregation. The third section concerns the preacher, for he is one of the people involved in the preaching event. The final section is a discussion of the message. The message grows out of the encounter between pastor and people at a particular time and in a particular place.

The basic point of view that is presupposed throughout this book is that preaching is an "event." It is a communication event. To isolate any element in this event is artificial. The elements in the event are congregation, preacher, and message. In virtually all the essays in this book I will be interweaving the elements, even though the essays are grouped into categories.

Let me illustrate this idea of preaching as an event.

A sermon can be rather poor in terms of logic, structure, etc., and yet the preaching event can be of real significance. Haven't you experienced occasions when merely to preach on a certain topic, regardless of what is said, was an event of significance? It often happens when the topic is a controversial one. Everyone is thinking about it. What the preacher says about the topic is important, but the fact that he deals with the topic is in and of itself significant. An example would be a sermon on fair housing when the community is divided on the issue.

The preacher is not the sole conditioner of the preaching event. It is not " his " sermon. What happens in the preaching event is determined only in part by what he says and who he is. A good many of the factors that determine the event are out of his control. For example, the mood of the congregation may have a powerful influence. Or the problems of the immediate community. Or the atmosphere of the sanctuary combined with the memories of past events that took place there. The preacher is one element in the event.

We could call the view of preaching that is delineated in this book " situational preaching." That sounds sufficiently *avant-garde*. Perhaps " contextual preaching " is another useful label. That sounds somewhat intellectual, or even academic. Frankly, I prefer to use the phrase " the preaching event." I am not convinced that it helps to give preaching a descriptive or delimiting adjective. Preaching is an event. It is, hopefully, a significant event.

Something should be said about the style of this book. Many of us have rather short attention spans. This may be a result, in part, of watching television. We are used to receiving timed segments of information. I find it difficult to sit down for a long period of time to read a nonfiction work. It is hard to follow a line of thought for page after page after page. We want an idea to " come through " to us as soon as possible. In fact, unless the author makes his point clearly and succinctly, we wonder if he knows what he means or cares that we know.

This book is a series of brief essays. None of them takes very long to read. Some of them are in soliloquy form, some are dialogues, others are straight discussions. There are a few transcripts of group discussions. I have used these various forms partly in order to hold the reader's interest, and partly because I enjoy writing in a variety of forms. It is my belief that the more familiar, the more lifelike, the writing style, the easier it will be to comprehend the meaning or meanings of the essays. I would imagine that this is not the kind of book a person would read in one sitting. In some ways, it is more of a reference work. Each essay stands alone, so the book can be picked up and opened to almost any spot and read with understanding.

I use ordinary language in the book. That is, I use colloquial American. I write the way I speak. This is not done out of condescension, nor for the benefit of the nonspecialist. I normally think, speak, and write in colloquial American. So why not do so in a book?

This book is intended for preachers, theological students, and anyone else in any congregation who thinks that the preaching event should be of significance. Have I left anyone out?

Finally, I have written from the point of view of a person who has been a layman a lot longer than he has been a pastor or a professor of preaching. I tend to write as a person who has sat in church pews for many, many hours and listened to a host of preachers. Some of them were very good, some very poor, and most were in-between. I have done a fair amount of preaching in my time. But mostly I have heard others preach. Preaching scares me to death when I think of the responsibility it entails. But I must confess that it is often a lot harder to listen to a preacher than it is for me to preach myself. I want desperately for this event to be of significance, and so often it is not. At least if I am preaching, I know who to blame if I fail.

The two essays " What Kind of Preaching Is Needed To-day " and " What Kind of Preachers Are Needed Today " were excerpted from " Preaching as Invitation," which appeared in *Central Baptist Seminary Journal,* Vol. I, No. 1 (February, 1966), and are used by permission.

I | A Rationale for the Preaching Event

THE QUESTION of rationale may be dealt with in two ways. First, from the standpoint of communication theory. Secondly, from the Biblical standpoint. The first essay in this chapter is based on my understanding of contemporary communication theory plus a very personal analysis of my own communication needs. The second essay (" A Reaction ") is an imaginary dialogue between myself and a person who would approach communication from a more self-consciously Biblical perspective. The final essay (" Because Jesus Preached ") is an attempt to combine the Biblical viewpoint with the insights of communication theory and show that there is no essential contradiction between the two.

Shall We in Fact Still Try to Communicate?

I have been struck by the way in which J. C. Hoekendijk, in his book *The Church Inside Out* (The Westminster Press, 1966), poses the question of what the church will do in the future.

It seems to me that we have to cultivate a healthy skepticism toward all traditional forms and procedures; we must prevent ourselves from being hypnotized by familiarity. Therefore we must put the fundamental questions: not begin halfway with the question " *How* shall we continue to do in the future what we used to do in Egypt? " (for instance, *how* shall we have to preach?), but we must begin to ask the basic question *whether* the dear old (and perhaps sacred?) way can and must be continued in the future ("shall we in fact still preach? "). (P. 178.)

The basic question we have to face is not *how* shall we preach or even *what* shall we preach but, Shall we in fact still preach? Is there any rationale at all for preaching? This question has been put off too often. Of course, it is easier and less personally threatening to learn techniques, clever ways of projecting your voice, gimmicks to use to catch the ear of the congregation, than it is to face the void. We can put off the question as to whether or not we should preach by preaching extremely well. Doing the job with efficiency can appear to be a valid excuse for doing it at all. "Obviously if you can do something well, it is worth doing." Isn't this a bit like saying that since the Nazis carried out the extermination of the Jews so efficiently, it must have been a job worth doing? Is efficiency its own excuse for being?

We need to assume at the outset that we are not encouraging or condoning poor preaching. Our answer to a question such as, Shall so many in fact do such a rotten job in the pulpit? is an unequivocal No. Incidentally, it is not very difficult to determine what is poor preaching. Ask any congregation. They will tell you. And they usually know long before their pastor does.

Our concern is with competent preaching. Shall we in fact still preach competently? Is it worth doing? Does it matter?

Allow me to put this question about preaching in a broader perspective. We so often isolate preaching from the broader task of communication. The primary question is not, Shall we in fact still preach? Rather, we need to face up to the significance of communication and ask, Shall we in fact still try to communicate? Isn't this the more basic question?

Communication is essential. Our living is interpersonal. Persons need to relate meaningfully to one another in order for there to be life. Is an isolated individual a real person? Perhaps a simple answer to that question would be, Everyone I know seems to need other people. This may be too simple an answer, but I find it satisfying. We need other people. How do we need them? In many ways — their presence, their touch, their acceptance and rejection, their looking at us and our looking at them, their "imaging" of us and our "imaging" of them. We've grown accustomed to their faces. It's "like breathing out and breathing in." Indeed, it is life itself. All of these ways of needing one another are ways of communicating. Presence is communication, touch is communication, acceptance and rejection are communication, looking is communication, "imaging" (if you let another in on your image of him) is communication. All of this reacting, feeling, thinking, judging, is communication. Without communication we are isolated, miserable, incomplete — less than persons.

Communication is, is it not, basic to our existence? It is impossible to survive in any livable way without it. Thus the answer to the question, Shall we in fact still try to communicate? is, We had better or we are dead.

Let us now make the connection between communication and preaching. May I be very personal at this point? It is difficult for me to communicate unless I can be, at least to some degree, confessional. Let me be confessional. I will list the kinds of communication I think I need and then relate these to preaching. I invite you to list your communication needs and see if they are in any way met in preaching.

1. *Recognition.* I need for another person to acknowledge

the fact that I am here and that I am a person who deserves to be considered. I want another to feel that I am worth recognizing. The preacher can help greatly in this respect. Isn't it possible to sense whether or not a preacher respects the congregation? I want the preacher to care that I am present. If he cares, he is saying to me that he knows my time is valuable and that he has no right to ask me to listen to him unless he knows that he has something to give. If I can feel that he respects me, then I receive recognition.

2. *Presence.* I feel the need of being in a group in which the participants are aware of one another's presence, a group that knows that it is " together." Part of this is a matter of sheer physical presence or closeness. There is touching. Usually the group is focused on something. In a group that is singing, the focus is on the song; the singing is communal, and as we sing we feel one another's nearness, we hear one another's voices, and we " tune in " on the vibrations from the other people in the group. Another example would be a sports event. Here we focus on what is happening on the floor or on the field. We all care about what happens. In regard to preaching, it seems to me that it is important for the preacher to call our attention to the " togetherness " of the congregation. He can tell us of the basis of our being together here in this place at this time. Are we a crowd or a community? an aggregation or a congregation? He can put our being together into perspective and help us to realize its meaning in more depth. It is also possible for him to challenge us in such a way that we feel that this group of people, because we are together, can accomplish more than we could in separation from one another.

3. *Listening.* It is important to me for another person to listen to me. This is particularly true if I am telling him about what is significant for me. I want him to respond to my telling. This response does not have to be limited to words. Facial

expressions, paying attention to me, are important responses. I want to know that what I am saying interests him and is thus judged by him to be worth listening to. I need to feel that he feels he can learn something from me. It is possible to tell if a preacher listens to people or not. This is particularly evident when he includes in his sermons references to the feelings of people, and the ideas of *other* people. I will listen to him if he shows respect for others, and if I know that he has listened deeply to people and not just to their voices. Then I know that he would listen to me, and that he, indirectly but actually, is listening to me even as he is preaching.

4. *Dialogue.* It is not necessary for me to hear only the echo of my own voice. I need to have someone speak to me of what is real to him, and for him to respond to my speaking to him of what is real to me. I want him to expect me to react to what he says and to who he is. There needs to be a mutual agreement that each of us can contribute to the other. I want his honest reaction, and not one that is geared to "helping" me or manipulating me. And I would hope that he would want honesty from me as well. The preacher needs to let me know whether or not he wants me to react to what he is saying. Not necessarily to react verbally, but possibly to react inwardly. If he speaks honestly and with a sense of urgency, but not as if he had the last word on the subject, then I sense that he is calling for my response. Unless he wants me to react, I do not care too much about what he is saying, and I would question whether he cares. Of course, it would help if he provided opportunities for verbal dialogue after his sermon. Then I could tell more clearly if he cared about me and my response.

5. *Contribution.* I want to know that I am needed, that my contribution is important to other people, and that there are people who recognize that they need what I have to give. When there are people who desire my presence and who call

upon me to use my talents, I find this quite satisfying. Unless I am needed, I feel useless and like an interchangeable part of a machine. The preacher can be of great help here. If, in his sermons, he lists the needs as he sees them and asks for people to meet these needs, he is doing me a favor. It is not too helpful when the preacher waxes moralistic and complains about how few people are working in the church. Rather, I am appreciative if he has taken the time to discover significant needs and if he obviously is really asking for help (not demanding it) — help that I could give voluntarily, and help that would really fit *my* talents and *my* concerns. I want the preacher to communicate to me the fact that I am needed.

6. *Therapy*. There is within me a need for another person to tell me something about myself. Not that I want everyone to do this. Either I have to ask this person to do so or I already have a relationship with him that is based on mutual trust and respect, and he volunteers such information within the context of this relationship. I want this person to tell me who I am from his point of view. It is also helpful if he allows me to tell him who I think he is. But that is not always necessary. In this telling me who I am, I do not want him to "lecture" me. He might draw out of me some admissions as to who I am. He might suggest some categories or names for who I am. Or he may tell me who he thinks he is, and this, in turn, stimulates me to tell him who I think I am. A preacher can do this in a general sense. That is, he can speak to the whole congregation about who he thinks we are. And he can share with us who he thinks he is. Group therapy in the context of the preaching event can be very effective, as witnessed in the preaching of Harry Emerson Fosdick or Leslie Weatherhead. I would also like to feel that the preacher would be open to a more personal therapy session — that I could go to him with my problems and that he would be able to help me. Preaching

can be a preparation for, or even a stimulus to, a more personal therapeutic relationship.

7. *Judgment.* I need to know people who take life seriously enough to criticize and even condemn and reject what they feel to be evil in this world. People who will " tell it like it is." This can be done in a group, but it can also be done individually. I need for someone to point out to me where he thinks I have gone " off the track." Of course, this must be a person who has earned my respect and the right to speak to me in this way. It is most helpful if the person who judges me is one who loves me and whom I love. I find that I want to be judged because I want to be taken seriously. A preacher can preach judgment. Particularly if he judges because he is taking life and people seriously. He should say what he feels and condemn what he thinks should be condemned. I appreciate this, as long as I know that he is not doing it merely to work off some personal frustration, out of viciousness or self-righteousness, or because he thinks that he ought to be judgmental in order to fit the image of what a preacher is supposed to be.

8. *Hope.* As I get older, I discover that I need more and more to hear from people who have lived life more deeply than have I — people who have known suffering and have found meaning in it, or in spite of it, or on the other side of it. I need to know what meaning a person such as Viktor Frankl has found, after spending years in Nazi death camps. I want to hear from people who have discovered hope in circumstances that would bring most of us to the depths of despair. Then I can have hope. I can know that hope can come, even when everything seems to work against it. I need to hear from a preacher who has lived deeply and who can bring the perspective of his life and experience to us in order that we may profit from it. At the very least, I need to hear him tell me of true experiences (not made-up stories) of people who have

found hope in the midst of despair. I need to know where I can find hope, and what can be done and believed in that will make life worthwhile.

9. *Commitment.* I need a person (and I think immediately of my wife) who will commit herself to living with me and loving me. This person must take me as I am, and pronounce me " good." I want a friend or friends who care about me and want me to care about them. I need a group of people who take me as a person who can give them something and who want to communicate with me — a group of people with whom I am joined in a common endeavor which we all acknowledge as important, valid, and life-giving. In other words, I need commitment — the commitment of another to me, the expectation of commitment from me, and the commitment of a group to a common goal and a common work. I think that the preacher must try to call forth from me and from all in the congregation a commitment of this kind. That is, a group commitment. But he must prove to us that it is a significant commitment. And he must communicate to me his willingness to be as committed as he expects me to be.

10. *Information.* I am very ignorant of so much that is important. Thus I need for people to tell me things I need to know. People need to give me information that I could not get out of a book, or would probably not try to. I want such people to care about the facts they are presenting, and to care about my caring about them. It may be that a person will tell me of an event that should be of interest to me. It helps if I can identify with the characters (or at least one of them) in this event. It is obvious that the preacher can provide me with the kind of facts of which I speak, and in a manner in which I need to receive them. He can give me facts about the Bible, the history of Christian thought and action, and about our present age, its needs and challenges, which can be of real help.

11. *Entertainment.* I like to see someone do something and do it well — to admire a performer's work, and to feel that he is giving his best for my benefit. When I see another person using his talents to their fullest extent, it makes me glad that I am a human being. Like the child who imitates the movie star — the child wants to show what he can do too. I find that I can project myself into the performance of another. I "lose" myself or at least I experience something through him that I would not otherwise experience. Thus, I am very pleased when a preacher uses his talents to the utmost — his voice, manner, energy, intelligence. He is showing respect for me by taking his craft seriously. I rejoice in his willingness to do his best. This kind of entertainment — the use of one's talents to the fullest extent — meets a real need.

12. *Solitude.* There are times when I want other people to leave me alone — to make no demands on me. I need people who respect my desire for solitude. I need people who are sensitive to my needs and who do not try to deal with me when I push them off. For that matter, I need people who want to be treated this way by me — people who want me to leave them alone at times. The preacher should respect my judgment. He should not condemn me if I refuse to follow his suggestions. In fact, I would hope that he would leave me alone to work out my own salvation. In other words, he should respect my ability and my wisdom.

Those are my twelve communication needs, or, at least, the only ones I can think of at this juncture in my life. I have tried to show how preaching can, to some degree, meet all of these needs. If I am correct, then preaching can be a means of valid and significant communication. Preaching can be one way of meeting many of my communication needs.

Shall we in fact still try to communicate? I should hope so, for without communication we would be unable to become

persons. Shall we in fact still preach? Yes, as long as we realize that our preaching must meet real needs, not manufactured
ones. If communication is essential, then preaching that communicates is also essential.

A Reaction

REACTOR: Aren't you still avoiding the central issue? So you
have the particular communication needs which you list —
and I thought you would never quit listing them. But how do
you know if these needs are valid or if the gospel is intended
to meet these needs? The question, it seems to me, is not what
needs you think you have (what do you know of yourself?),
but what needs the gospel is geared to meet. Or, to put it even
more authoritatively, what does God say that you and I need?
Isn't this more important than a description of your own feelings?

AUTHOR: Unless the preacher who preaches what he conceives
to be the gospel speaks to needs that I personally feel, I don't
care how orthodox or theologically correct he may be — he
doesn't communicate. Not only that, but I feel that all the
communication needs I have listed are perfectly valid, even in
the light of what the gospel says about our living. To be sure,
Christians have defined and redefined such terms as presence,
dialogue, judgment, hope, etc. The descriptions I give are not,
in my view, unchristian. No doubt I am greatly influenced in
my selection by my Christian background.

REACTOR: But preaching is generally considered to be the presenting or re-presenting of the revelation of God in Jesus
Christ. It is not primarily the meeting of communication needs
as defined by the congregation. The preacher preaches be-

cause there is a revelation and because people need to know this revelation for their own salvation.

AUTHOR: The revealing of God is done through the meeting of man's communication needs. It is not primarily a matter of revealing a body of knowledge. It is a matter of making God known to us in our living, of God's making our brother known to us and making his needs known to us. Salvation comes as we serve our brothers and sisters in the light of God's revealing of them to us and granting us the power and the wisdom to be of help. God doesn't throw us an idea; he sends us on a mission.

REACTOR: You think that these communication needs which you list are given to you by God?

AUTHOR: All right.

REACTOR: These needs constitute your openness to his revealing?

AUTHOR: O.K. However, there is a " dark side " to these needs which I have listed. They can constitute both an openness and a resistance. The need for recognition also involves a desire to gain power over people. The need for presence involves the desire to be completely " other-directed " by the group — to sacrifice my freedom. The need for dialogue includes a desire to escape from service into talking. The need for judgment includes a kind of self-torturing. Each one of these needs stands in need of correction and of the grace of God and the judgment of him and of my fellow human beings.

REACTOR: Shouldn't the preacher speak to your tendency to succumb to the " dark side " of your communication needs? This might be one of his primary jobs.

AUTHOR: I would hope so — though it would not make him very popular. However, it might help to make him a preacher.

Because Jesus Preached

The usual rationale for preaching, reduced to its simplest form, is that we do it because Jesus did it. Or, more broadly, because the Bible calls for preaching. Isn't this the basic Christian rationale for preaching? Jesus did it, his disciples did it, so we are supposed to do it.

But why did Jesus preach? And what kind of preaching did he do?

It would seem that Jesus preached to people because he believed that they needed to see their lives in perspective. They needed to know what their lives " meant." The kind of preaching he did was the kind that gave perspective to their living.

Jesus showed the people of his time how they could see their living in the perspective of the oral and written ideas of men who were sensitive to God's presence and directing. In other words, he used what we call the Old Testament to put the first century A.D. into perspective. He did this, for example, in the so-called Sermon on the Mount. In so doing, he criticized certain interpretations of the Law and the Prophets and brought some of their insights up-to-date. Jesus also used parables to help put people's lives into perspective — to get their living into focus. He invited people to look at common occurrences and to understand their meaning — that is, to dig deeply into the significance of everyday activities. Jesus interpreted the " signs of the times." The disciples were being hounded by their enemies — What does this mean? People were being healed — What does this mean? The Roman government was oppressing the people — What does this mean? Finally, Jesus preached by calling people to action. He told them, for example, that they should reject much that is called "religion" and focus on works of love and justice. He told some of them to give all they had to those in need. He told others to heal their fellowmen. And Jesus even told some to be more religious.

Jesus preached because he wanted people to see their lives in the perspective of God's will and their brothers' needs. He preached because he wanted people to connect what was happening in the first century A.D. with God's past work with his people. Jesus preached because people needed to discern the meaning of everyday occurrences and they also needed to interpret the signs of their time. He preached in order to spur men on to service. Always he preached to men's needs. Not always to the needs they said they felt — needs such as adhering to the law's letter and thereby gaining security, or needs such as a military victory for Israel, or needs such as wreaking vengeance on their economic oppressors, or needs such as finding an easy life and still being right with God. These kinds of needs he condemned. Jesus focused on men's true needs.

Why preach? Because Jesus did? Not necessarily. But for the same reasons that Jesus did. Our living, our time, needs to be put into perspective. We need the light that God is supposed to bring. Not that we will get it in one blinding flash. Not that we will suddenly see our lives in clear perspective, but in order that we will have at least a candle and will not be content to curse the darkness — in order that in the midst of the dark wood there will be a little clearing. Nor are we merely to try to make sense of our own living. For we need to see our brother's living in a new light — a light that we can bring to him. We preach to shed light, to give perspective, to call men and women to action, to spur them on and give them hope.

It has been said that Jesus' central message was that the Kingdom of God has come. Can it be our message that God has come in our time? Is it our task to try to see where and how he has come? And perhaps to see to whom he has come and is coming? In our time, we need to learn how to follow in the footsteps of the One who is hidden as well as manifest — who, even in his seeming absence, has left a trace, a print to decipher, a blaze on a tree, a wisp of a cloud by day, and a flickering candle by night.

II | *The Congregation and the Preaching Event*

It is time that we faced up to how people feel about the preaching they hear. Preaching is not true communication unless something happens to the congregation. In this chapter, I identify with the congregation. I am trying to present what I have felt as a member of the congregation, what I have heard others say that they felt, and what I have sensed in others, though they have not always been so outspoken as I have tried to be.

The first essay is not a transcript of an actual lay criticism session, but a partly fictionalized, partly remembered account of a couple of sessions. These sessions followed sermons by students at our seminary. I moderated the sessions and the lay participants were selected by the students from the congregations they served. In the selecting of the participants a conscious attempt was made to get as representative a group as possible. The criterion for selection was *variety*—variety in ages (senior high to elderly), educational background, levels of sophistication, and theological viewpoints. It has been my experience that such selectivity is essential to the success of the session.

The second essay ("Respect") is a very personal, and rather

angry indictment of a great deal of preaching that I have heard. The essay on "Speaking to Individuals" is something of a continuation of this indictment, on a different but related theme. "Those Are Real People in There" reflects the feelings of many people with whom I am acquainted — particularly those adults who were saturated with Bible lessons when they were young, but never really understood what was happening until much later. In the essays on "Identification" and "Simplicity" I try to identify with different types of people and comment on what is happening to them. I imagine that in the "Dialogue on Success and Failure" it is obvious that my sympathies are with B and that he speaks for me to a much greater extent than does A. And yet I think that A is a real person, and not merely a foil for B. "What People Want" is my own analysis of the varieties of people in a congregation. It is a summary statement of what people think they want from the preacher. The final essay on "Lay Preaching" is a personal plea for allowing lay witness to occur.

Listen to the congregation. If you are a layman, I imagine you will identify with many of them. If you are a preacher, you may feel personally threatened. I can sympathize with both reactions.

A Lay Criticism Session

MODERATOR: First of all, let me ask any of you who are willing to tell me what Fred said to you personally. I don't mean the theme of the sermon necessarily, but what you got out of it. What was the main thing that came through to you?

Woman: I thought the main thing he said was that we need to get personally involved in social issues. We can't just let other people do for us what we should be doing.

Man: I got something like that out of it, but a little bit different. I got the idea that it isn't just personal evangelism that is important, not just winning souls for Christ, but taking care of the bodies of men and women too. You know, taking care of their physical needs.

Man: I don't know, I guess I got something quite different out of it. I thought he was saying that the church shouldn't let the government do what the church should be doing. The government has taken over too many of the things that churches used to do. We ought to start doing them again. In the name of Jesus — not like some social agency would.

MODERATOR: It is interesting to see that different people get somewhat different ideas out of the same session. Maybe we hear what interests us most. Some of us probably take a point out of the sermon and then sort of write our own sermons.

Woman: Well, I think I was really hit by his point about getting personally involved. I find it hard to do that.

(The sermon which the laymen are criticizing was based on the account of the Last Judgment in Matt., ch. 25. One of the points that the preacher made was the need for personal involvement in social issues. Another was the need for refusing to let the government do everything. However, the main point, in the thinking of the preacher, was that when you do something for people in need, you serve Christ in a literal sense — this person in need is Christ to you. None of the people in the lay criticism group spoke of this as a theme — at least not in these words.)

MODERATOR: Now that we have brought out some of the main points in the sermon, let's get to a somewhat stickier matter. To put it bluntly, did you feel that it was worth your while to be here this morning? Are you glad you came to hear Fred, or did you hear something you have heard before, the same old stuff, and you really didn't get too much out of it — at least nothing new?

Man: I have heard what he said before, but it helps to hear it again. Maybe if we hear it often enough, we will do something about it.

Woman: Well, I'll be frank — and this is nothing against Fred personally — but I feel that we hear this kind of thing all the time. What I want is for someone to tell me what we are supposed to do about it.

MODERATOR: You didn't feel that Fred was specific enough about what he wanted you to do?

Woman: That's right. I know what the problems are. What are the answers?

Man: That's a good point. I don't think he was specific enough. Maybe if he could have related what he said to our church here. What can we do here in this church?

MODERATOR: Do you think that Fred has a responsibility to give specific suggestions?

Woman: Oh, definitely. If he won't, then who will?

Man: Well, I don't agree with that altogether. I think the preacher should kind of give us the theory, what the Bible says, and then we should find ways of applying it. *We* are the church, after all, and we need to look at what the Bible says and then say what this means for us.

MODERATOR: You don't think Fred needs to spell it out too much?

Man: We ought to be able to spell it out. That is why we have boards and committees.

Man: Not only that, but Fred isn't with us on our jobs. He doesn't know how to spell it out for us where we work all day. We have to figure that out for ourselves.

Woman: You asked a while back if we thought it was worth our while to be here this morning. I have heard Fred preach better sermons. I frankly didn't think this was one of his best ones. But I do think that I needed to hear what he said this morning. I also think that this discussion we are having shows that we got something out of his sermon. I think he made us all think. That's the main thing anyway, isn't it?

MODERATOR: It certainly is important, all right. Now let's get on to something else. This is not so much on the content of the sermon as on the presentation. You all know Fred pretty well. Did you feel that it was really Fred who was coming through to you this morning, or did you feel that he has a kind of "pulpit personality"? Did you feel that this was the "pulpit Fred" and not quite the real Fred?

Man: I wish he had smiled more. He really is not as solemn as he was in the pulpit.

Woman: Yes, but preaching is a pretty serious business. He should be serious about what he is saying.

Man: Serious, yes. But he can relax a little more. Maybe he was a little "shook up" because he knew we were going to criticize him.

Man: Fred is a serious guy, too, though. I felt that he was really getting to us. I didn't feel that he needed to be humorous or tell jokes.

Woman: Not humorous like telling jokes. But a little more relaxed. It is easier to accept criticism from a preacher if he doesn't just pound it out, if he doesn't push hard all the time.

MODERATOR: Do the rest of you feel that Fred was being himself?

Man: He was like he is sometimes. But he is really more personable most of the time. When he is at the house he loosens up a lot more. I think he is basically friendlier than he was in the pulpit.

Woman: But preaching is a serious business. I want the preacher to be serious.

Man: I think Fred has a very warm personality. I didn't think he was too warm this morning.

MODERATOR: Should he have been more conversational?

Woman: That's it. More conversational. More like he was talking to each one of us personally rather than to a big group. I felt he was preaching to a group, but not so much to me personally.

Man: But he *is* preaching to a group. It isn't like he was in your living room.

Woman: But shouldn't it be like he was in a living room? Wouldn't this have a more powerful effect on us?

Man: I don't see anything wrong even with being humorous once in a while. We need for him to let up a little bit and then drive a point home. You know, soften us up and then let go with what he wants us to hear.

MODERATOR: Let's push on to this matter of speech delivery. What about his voice? Is it easy to listen to?

Man: Oh, yes, I can hear him very well. He has a good voice.

Woman: Sometimes I think he is too easy to listen to. I get carried away with his voice and don't always hear what he says.

MODERATOR: Is his voice monotonous?

Woman: There isn't as much variety as there should be. He is kind of on the same pitch most of the time.

Man: Maybe he should be more dramatic.

Woman: I think he needs to pause more. He speaks too fast. I have trouble keeping up with him sometimes.

Woman: Sometimes he drops his voice at the end of a sentence, and I don't quite get what he says. He did that at the end of his sermon, and I missed the last couple of words.

Man: At the end, he stopped too suddenly. I wasn't ready for him to stop yet. I need to be built up to a climax and instead he just dropped me.

Woman: But he said what he had to say. I don't feel he had to end it with a flourish necessarily.

MODERATOR: Would it have helped if he had done more summarizing at the end?

Woman: Not summarizing so much. I know what he said. But I do think he needed to end with a challenge. Something positive.

Man: I really don't think Fred uses his voice as well as he could. When he speaks normally, he uses more emphasis than he does in the pulpit. I mean he has more variety. When he is in the pulpit, he lets his voice get kind of impersonal.

MODERATOR: Does he have a pulpit tone?

Man: Not a pulpit tone like the old evangelistic preachers. But a pulpit voice which is not just like his normal voice.

Woman: I didn't have any trouble hearing him. He projects. And that isn't easy in our church's sanctuary.

Man: I would like for him to pause more and let what he says have time to sink in.

MODERATOR: Is there any comment anyone wants to make that they didn't get a chance to?

Woman: I would like to say that Fred needs to be less tied down to his notes. He needs to get with the congregation more, to look at us more, to be freer.

Man: I felt he was speaking to a certain group in the congregation. More to the young people and young adults and middle-aged. Not much to the older people. Some of the older people might have felt left out.

Woman: Well, I am an older person, I guess. I thought he was talking right to me. I don't think we are that much different from the rest of you.

Man: I think because he is younger though that he particularly relates to younger people.

Woman: I would like to say that Fred really has an ability to say what he thinks and to say it clearly. You don't have any trouble trying to find out what he has said. I like that. He "calls a spade a spade."

Man: We have been kind of hard on Fred. I think we all appreciate his preaching. I hope he doesn't think we've been unnecessarily critical.

MODERATOR: I am sure that he wants to know what you think. After all, he is preaching to *you,* and if you don't get what he is saying, then he might as well quit.

Respect

If I were to focus on the one thing that I want most from a preacher in terms of his attitude toward me, I would say that that one thing is *respect.* I want him to respect me.

I do not want a preacher to attack me. He has no right to do that — even if he speaks in God's name. No preacher has earned the right to attack me. For that matter, I can't really think of anyone who has earned the right to attack me. My wife, perhaps, but she doesn't actually attack me. Criticize,

fine, but attack? No. When a preacher attacks me, he is refusing to treat me with respect. Yet some preachers have vi-
ciously attacked me, not me as an individual, singled out in
a congregation, but me as a part of a congregation. If the
preacher is sick, let him attack his psychiatrist.

I do not want a preacher to act as if I *should* be in the congregation. As if I am expected to be there — like it was the
basic duty of my existence. Rather, he should respect me
enough to want to show me, indeed, *prove* to me, that it is
worth my time and effort to be in the congregation. I think
he should be saying to me, though not in words but in attitude, that he is glad I am here this Sunday morning, that he
hopes that he has something to say that will challenge me, and
that if I am not challenged, he feels that it is mainly his fault.
In a way, he has invited me to come and hear him. He should
take me seriously enough — show me enough respect — to
make it worth my time and effort.

I cannot stand to have a preacher talk down to me, as if I
were stupid or " unspiritual " or religiously illiterate. As if he
were the expert on religious matters and I were a novice. To
be sure, he may know more about some religious matters than
I do, but I doubt very much that he is any wiser about the
things in life that really matter than am I. He is a man and
I am a man. There is no basic difference between us. Furthermore, I resent it when a preacher will expect me to feel some
kind of loyalty to him personally — as if I am leading such an
insignificant life that loyalty to him because of his office is an
important and necessary ingredient of my life. My life is not
all that dull, that I need such a loyalty to give it meaning. If
I have time to spare to please the preacher, then I must be
using my time poorly.

Finally, what I want to say is that I want a preacher who
takes his job seriously and who takes the congregation seri-

ously — a preacher who senses his tremendous responsibility, who is a steward of his time and of the time which he is asking us to take to listen to him. If he has nothing to say, may he respect us enough to admit it. If he has something to say, may he respect us enough to say it, to say it well, and to say it in love.

Speaking to Individuals

A woman was criticizing the preacher: "I didn't feel that he was conscious of me as an individual — I felt he was preaching to a group, to a mass of people, but not to any of us as individuals." What did she mean?

I have had the feeling at times that some preachers think of congregations as interchangeable. It could be this congregation or some other congregation. It doesn't make any difference. For the preacher it is the sermon, the written or memorized words that matter, and not the people out in front. He is preaching to a group, not to these people.

Another kind of problem is the preacher who is afraid of the congregation. He hides behind the pulpit. He hides behind his words. He is like a tape recorder. His tape plays, but he doesn't really need to have been there. In fact, I get the feeling that he would rather he was not there. And I agree with him — I would rather he wasn't there either. I could get the same ideas from reading a book. Actually I would read a better book.

Or haven't you known a preacher as an individual and then when he gets behind the pulpit, you hardly recognize him? He puts on a different personality. It may not be an obnoxious personality. Actually, it may be a rather pleasing personality. But it is not the man you and I know. We feel that he is a stranger, and that either he has not been giving his real self to us when he is among us, or he is "putting us on" while he is in the pulpit. He does not come through as the man who we thought he was.

There are preachers who preach to people as groups. They are constantly referring to " the people who . . ." or " the kind of person who . . ." They never seem to think of individuals as individuals but only of " types " — individuals who lose their individuality by being subsumed under a category. I have sometimes felt safe and comfortable when I listened to such a preacher, because I never seemed to fit into any of the groups he mentioned. However, I also felt cheated, because he did not deal with me at all.

The woman who wanted the preacher to recognize her as an individual wanted to know that he cared enough about her to deal with her. Not that she expected him to come down out of the pulpit and shake her hand. But she wanted him to come into the pulpit as if he were coming into her living room — with concern, with his real personality, with humility, and with an interest in communicating with her — as a guest.

Those Are Real People in There

" What a shock! It just hadn't hit me before. Those are real people in there! All those Bible characters. All that stuff they gave us in Sunday school. All those characters in beards and sheets, and holding shepherd's crooks. They were real people. How about that?

" I always thought the Bible was about fairy-tale people. Miracles and voices from the sky and seas parting and suns stopping. Fantastic. The stories had morals, but that was about it. Even Jesus never seemed quite human to me. He was a perfect, sinless, noble, godlike figure — going around preaching and doing miracles — but not a real person.

" Then I heard this preacher. He talked about Jesus and his

problems with the disciples — how one man wanted to get in on a good thing because he was a disciple, and his brother felt the same way. So Jesus bawled them out and said that they had no more right than anyone else to get their way. And besides, they should be concerned about giving rather than getting. Jesus acted real human. I know people like those two brothers. In fact, I am a lot like them. I think, like the preacher said, that because of all the good things I've done I deserve some kind of special recognition — some special treatment. But if I am doing good things only so that I can get special treatment, I'm not really doing anything good, am I? Though the preacher also said that God knows that we do things for a lot of reasons. It isn't something to ignore or deny, that we do things to get ahead. We just ought to face up to it and be honest about it and ask ourselves if there are any other reasons — other reasons like doing something to help someone, or doing something that would make us feel like we were doing something worthwhile even if no one knew about it or thanked us. Jesus was pretty realistic about human nature. I would say that he was at least human enough to know what human beings are like.

"If I can find out something about myself from reading the Bible, then it would be worth it to read it. If it isn't just a bunch of fairy stories, maybe I could get something out of it. I could see myself in it or see how Jesus would deal with me or what Paul would say about me or even what the Old Testament prophets would say to me. This could get interesting."

Identification

[1] . . . If I sit far enough back, I won't have to pay attention and he will never notice. . . . There he is, with that usual phony grin. Like he is asking, "Please accept me, please ap-

plaud me, please say you need me." He's my pastor, I don't want to have to be his. . . . Actually, I don't like to think of him as *my* pastor. I would never go to him if I had a real problem. He is nothing but one big problem himself. . . . Here we go with the prayer. Just the right words. So glib. I wouldn't mind praying, if he didn't keep getting in the way. . . . Those announcements. So friendly. Not friendly, folksy. What does he think we are, a bunch of hicks? . . . Boy, is it ever hard to worship in here. He keeps getting in the way. I don't know quite what it is, but I just cannot stand his personality. . . . When Mary's mother died, he came to see Mary. And Mary couldn't stand him, kept wishing he would leave. I can understand that. I hope he never calls on me. . . . Time for the sermon. . . . I wish I could get by with bringing a book or even a church school paper, like the kids do. Right now I would like to be reading *Time* magazine or maybe looking at *Look*. That would be relaxing. What a week I had last week! What I need is relaxation. . . . I think he just told a joke. Some of the people are snickering. That is all we need — jokes. . . . Oh, a sermon on love. A lot he knows about love. I wonder what his wife could tell us about what he knows about love. I'll bet he is a lousy lover. . . . Love your neighbor as yourself. If we had love in our hearts, we could. If we had the love of Jesus. Sure. How many times have I heard that? It's all right. But so what? Go ahead, name a neighbor. You don't have the guts to do that, do you? Do you know what it is like to love the neighbor who lives next to me? His dog keeps coming over into our yard. That mutt. Sometime I am going to poison that dog. . . . How long is this going to go on? . . . I wonder if Sam and Doris are going to be home this afternoon? . . .

[2] . . . Nice sanctuary. Comfortable, relaxing. Easy to go to sleep. Though I hear that this man is a good preacher. . . . Nice prayer. Well put together. Done with precision. Not sweet

or gushy. . . . Good crisp job of announcements. No extras. Just the important things. . . . I may like this. . . . He reads Scripture well. Doesn't drag it. Doesn't overdo it either. . . . Sounds like an interesting topic. . . . Yes, I agree, that is a problem. I find it hard to know what is wrong and what is right too. . . . Good point. . . . Pretty forceful speaker. Good and clear. . . . I kind of have a funny feeling, though. It is almost like he is not talking to me or even to anyone here. It is like he is talking into a microphone. To people out there. . . . It is well put together and interesting. And the words are well chosen. But does he care about us — me, for example? . . . He is interesting to listen to. I wonder if he is on the radio? If he is, then I could stay home and get the same thing. . . .

[3] . . . That service wasn't much. Maybe the sermon will amount to something. . . . I don't know why he has laymen leading the service. They aren't very competent. I like a little more efficiency. . . . What is he talking about? Reconciliation? Good luck! . . . Does he have that problem too? I thought I was the only one. He can't get along with that kind of people either, huh? . . . Yeah, how *do* you deal with them? . . . I'm not sure I want to pay that kind of a price to get along with George and Mike. Yeah, I know it isn't going to be easy. I know that Christianity says that suffering is necessary. But isn't that an awful lot to ask? . . . You mean you think I can? Why? But you're different. You must be more religious than I am. Though I am not sure you are. You really know, don't you? You know what it is like. . . . Maybe you're right. Maybe I can. I'll give it a try. . . .

You can turn off a preacher by thinking of him as someone about whom you can make a decision. I can turn someone off if he is way out there or over there or if he seems to be in a world of his own, even though he appears to be in the sanctuary with me. But there are some preachers I cannot turn off. For a very simple reason — they are there with me. I find it hard to turn someone off if he is in the same room with me, looking in my eyes and asking for my response. In the first example [1], the preacher had an obnoxious personality. But he also was unbelievable. He did not seem to be a person — a man. I could turn him off. The second preacher [2] was a technician. He was clever, but I could " watch " his performance. I could admire him, but he was not " with " me. The third preacher [3] demanded something of me. He identified with me. I entered into silent dialogue with him. It is as if he were in my living room, sharing with me. I cannot turn him off. That would be like walking out of the door and leaving my guest alone. Identification.

Simplicity

Pro: I like the Reverend's ability to put things simply. And he is dead right. Religion really is simple. All you have to do is trust God and believe that everything will come out all right. Just have faith. After all, Christ came that we might have life and have it abundantly. If we have faith in him, we will have eternal life. It is great, wonderful, and so simple. I don't see why some people want to mess it up with complicated theories. Those people who say that as Christians we need to take a stand on war and race and open housing — Jesus never worried about things like that. He talked about spiritual things — how to get right with God. So many people try to make Jesus into some kind of social reformer. That complicates it unnecessarily. Race and war are things we have to deal with to be sure. But I think the government is doing the best job it can. I mean, who am I to tell them what to do? I do my job and pray and go to church and try to get right with God. That's it. It isn't as complicated as some people make it out to be.

Con: He makes it all sound so simple. As if somehow it was easy to live in this world. Christ is the answer. Love your neighbor. Beef up your devotional life. Come to church. Read your Bible. That doesn't buy the groceries, buddy. I have to make a living. I have to try to get along with Tom and Jack and Hank, and I can't stand Tom, but I have to lick his boots or I won't keep my job. I hate Jack's guts, but he hands out the promotions. Hank " turns me off " completely with that " I've been around a hell of a lot longer than you have, buddy, and I know " attitude, but I have to work with him — I haven't any choice. Christ is the answer to this? Christ doesn't have anything to do with it. I know I should love these guys. But I can't love someone who could care less how I feel about him. And besides, " love " sounds a little " fruity " when it comes to dealing with my fellow males. I don't " love " Hank. I love my wife. Sure I feel guilty about hating these guys. But I would feel a whole lot guiltier if I quit this job and couldn't buy the groceries. I made it this far and I'll continue to make it. After all, I love my wife and kids and I have a responsibility to them.

Pastor's Wife: Jack seems to be getting more withdrawn. He is moving farther away from me. I don't know what to do about it. He seems serene and happy in his work, moving among the people and helping them. But he isn't home much. I hate to bother him when he is home. I'm sure he has so much on his mind — though he doesn't seem worried. I might as well admit it — I'm sick of this town. There is no one for the children to play with who are really up to the standard that I like. And so many of their friends have more money than we do and have things they don't need. The parents have no sense. The teachers here just aren't able to control the students and don't have the values we have. I want to get out of this town! But Jack seems happy here. I'm sure he is. I don't know what's wrong with me. Cindy says I'm crabby these days. "You sure are crabby, Mommy." But I'm not crabby, I just want what's right. Oh, Jack seems to think everything is fine. "It will all work out," he says. I suppose it will. I wish I had his faith. It must be wonderful. Though I don't see that he is really a better person than I am. I shouldn't think that. I should be more humble. I don't know what's wrong with me this morning. Maybe the closing hymn will help.

Dialogue on Success and Failure

A: I can't understand why you don't like Dr. Martin's preaching.

B: And I can't understand why you think he's so great.

A: It's very simple. I like the fact that he is always calling our attention to the positive side of life. He tells us what we can do, what we can accomplish. I get so sick of preachers who deal only with the seamy side of life, with sin and with how horrible everything is. I like a ray of light from the pulpit. I want to be shown that something can happen. I want the preacher to tell me where I can do something that will do some one some good. If preachers would concentrate on the positive, then we would all do more good. Just show us what needs to be done. That's what Dr. Martin does and that's why I think he is great.

B: What you like is just what I don't like. Martin is very American. The great American belief in success. Things are going to be better and better — onward and upward. He shows you how to be a success in religion, how to be a successful Christian, just like someone else might show you how to be a successful salesman or a successful shoe clerk. If there is one thing I don't want, it is a success-seller — certainly not in the pulpit.

A: But don't you want to be a success as a Christian?

B: A lot of times I wish I was, but I know damn well I can't be. You can't be a shining success in what counts in life. No one can. We don't need to learn how to be successful; we need to find out how to deal with failure. In the major challenges of life, all of us fail.

A: That's pretty pessimistic. I think I have been reasonably successful in a lot of things — like as a husband and father, for example.

B: Then you are either incredibly naïve or terribly insensitive. I have failed over and over again with my family. I don't really know how to give myself fully to my wife. I don't know how to treat the kids as unique individuals. I don't even know how to deal with my anger at them. I have failed in a lot of important ways.

A: You have no right to read your failures into my life. If I think I have been successful, I ought to know. And I don't like to be called naïve and insensitive. My feelings can get hurt too, you know. And I am as smart as the next guy.

B: Sure you can get your feelings hurt — like you just got them hurt right now. But can you be *deeply* hurt? Would you let yourself get deeply hurt? Did you ever allow your wife to tell you how she really feels about you — particularly when she is deep-down mad at you?

A: That wouldn't do any good. Everyone knows you build a relationship by emphasizing the positive. You look for the good in the other person, and you build him up — you don't tear him down. Like Dr. Martin says. I remember one time I went to him because I was having some problems with my boss down at work and Dr. Martin did me a world of good. He pointed out to me how I could look for the good in my boss, and think of the positive side of his personality. I tried it and it worked wonders.

B: Oh, I am sure it did. And I'm sure that you have valiantly suppressed all those hatreds, all those bad feelings you had toward your boss. You probably even feel guilty about ever having felt that way. And now you fit in, like a cog in a machine and go on your way rejoicing. Good for you. Good old successful machine. " Nice doggy."

A: I can't talk to you. You're mean and vicious. I try to look for some good in you, some positive things. I try to get along with you, but you are making it awfully hard for me.

B: Really? Can't you be successful at it? I am sure that I have some " positive " qualities if you only look deep enough. I would say, in fact, that the most positive quality I have is that I try to say what I think the way I think it. I match my words with my feelings. And this isn't easy. I feel guilty lots of times about expressing my true feelings. But I have to do it, in order to live with myself. I have to admit that I fail miserably at human relationships. But I don't know anyone who doesn't, at least to some degree. Including you.

A: I am not going to let this conversation degenerate into a fight between us. Let's get back to Dr. Martin's sermons. Don't you think he is right in saying that the Christian gospel is essentially positive?

B: I don't know. I really am not too concerned about what the Christian gospel is or is not. I am concerned about what life is. I am desperately concerned about my own life and its meaning and about the lives of those around me — particularly those who are close to me. If the Christian gospel gives me a way of handling life's successes and that's it, then I don't need it. I don't know many real successes. But if the Christian gospel gives me a way of dealing with my failures, then I will consider it.

A: One of the major points of the gospel is that failure can be turned into success. "Victorious living." Look at Paul. He was a failure as a person — a killer of Christians — but Jesus turned him around and made a man out of him. What a success story that is!

B: Is it? I've read some of Paul's letters. It seems to me that he lived on the edge of failure all the time. He had a desperate need to be delivered from the fear of death. He would say that he was delivered, and then he would wonder. He wanted to be a successful church builder, but the churches he started were full of hypocrites and people who couldn't stand Paul and who happily kept to their old ways. He wanted to be a martyr, and yet he didn't want to die. I would imagine that he was often a very miserable person — so I can identify with him. I can also identify with Peter. He wanted to follow Jesus and be the kind of man Jesus wanted him to be. Yet when his first big test came, he denied his master. I can understand that. More than once I have betrayed my friends by not standing up for them or by not being there when they needed me.

A: But Paul was a success. He started church after church and they have lasted over the centuries. Sure Peter failed once when he denied Jesus, but then he became a great and successful leader. And look at what the Christian religion has accomplished over the years.

B: Look, indeed. Look at how Christianity has deepened prejudices throughout the centuries. Look at the killings in the name of Christ, the witch-burnings, the heresy hunts, the Crusades, the slaughter of the hated Christ killers — the six million Jews in Europe. What a success story!

A: But you can't blame the killings and the burnings and the slaughter of the Jews on the gospel. That is unfair. The gospel doesn't call for that kind of thing.

B: No, but Christians have. The killings and the burnings

were done in Christ's name. One of the basic excuses for killing the Jews was the charge of deicide. To be sure, this work was not done by people we like, not done by people we want to identify with. But still done in Jesus' name or else out of a Christian heritage.

A: We should look at the positive things that Christianity has done — the transformation of previously evil lives, the development of social concern, the rise of a modern civilized society.

B: My friend, I am afraid that you and I are guilty of the same crime. We blame either failure or success on a religion. But it is not a religion that does these things — good or bad. It is human beings. And human beings do not know what is right or wrong. We act like children and like adults, often in the same moment. We are vicious and compassionate, all at once. This is the kind of human being I am. I know there are others like me. I want all of us to stick together, to comfort each other a bit, to look each other in the face, in fear and in love.

A: I can't be so pessimistic or fatalistic. I just can't.

B: Then I will cry for you, because you cannot face up to your own humanity. I will cry for all of us who resent being on this earth as human beings and not as gods. I will hope that we may either be given, or renew within ourselves, the strength to get through each day, to rebel against, and yet accept, death and evil and joy and the murder of a brother and the birth of a son. I will cry out for all of us who know we fail and who nonetheless get up each morning and go through it all once more. I will thank God for every precious person and for every precious day in which we live. I am glad that I am human. But I don't know how to live with it.

What People Want

There are so many different people in a congregation. If a preacher hoped to " give the people what they want," he would be faced with a hopeless task. In fact, it is absurd to think that one sermon, or years of sermons, or one preacher, or many preachers, could meet all of the needs, satisfy all the desires of all kinds of people. Let me illustrate this point by briefly describing fourteen kinds of desires that people have when they come to a worship service. Many of these desires are found in the same person, though the desires are often contradictory.

1. Some people are crying out for direction and guidance — not necessarily for guidance from the preacher, unless they consider him their authority. They want guidance from the One who supposedly put this world together. These people want to know how to put their lives together, and they want the One who drew up the " blueprints " to let them know.

2. Many men and women want inspiration, a lift, an injection of power or strength. They want a stimulant, something that helps them to go on living. Perhaps they need courage, or, at least, they need another person to expect them to be courageous.

3. Aren't there a large number of people who want peace, security, serenity, and comfort? They are afraid when everything appears to be a "jumbled mess." These people do not want more and more darkness, even cleverly analyzed darkness. They want light — preferably a light in which they can bask. They want to be filled with the radiance of tranquillity.

4. So many people in our time want to be wanted. They want to feel that they can contribute something, to know that other people are genuinely interested in what they have to offer.

5. Don't you know people who want a religion that is undemanding? Something that certifies as another acceptable

leisure-time activity. Religion can be put into a category — the religious category. Since what they want is a neat, complete, well-rounded existence, a little bit of religion helps round them out.

6. Of course, there are also those who want a demanding religion — a religion that requires their complete devotion. They like to feel " used," " drained." They want a " cross " to carry.

7. Many people are easily bored. They cannot stand to hear and see the same old things Sunday after Sunday, year after year. They do not feel involved in what is happening in the service. It is boring. It is " out there " or " up there," and they can take it or leave it. What they want is action. They want to be " involved."

8. We all know people who are religious dilettantes. They want to sniff, and perhaps even taste, religion, but certainly not eat it and definitely not digest it. These people get their " kicks " from weird liturgies, aesthetic thrills — anything that is out of the ordinary. Give them something different and they are happy.

9. A number of people today are afraid, panicked, scared to death by life. Life is too much for them. They live on the brink — the abyss. Any moment they think that they will plunge to their doom. Death may come or some tragedy will befall them. It will all be over in an instant. They need hope — certain hope right now.

10. Some people believe in nothing. They particularly do not believe in themselves. They cannot believe that anything is worth doing, or that anything can happen that is of real significance. These people want evidence to the contrary, but they probably wouldn't accept it as valid.

11. Have you noticed that most people seem to know a lot less about the Bible and theology than does the preacher? Even if they have memorized parts of the Bible, they do not seem to

understand what they have memorized. Theology is assumed to be something for specialists. They might like to hear more about the Bible and theology, but they would not necessarily accept what the preacher says.

12. There are people who want to be "talked down to." They like to feel little and insignificant. They rejoice in saying, "Woe is me, I am nothing." Somehow this seems to them to help them deal with their guilt.

13. Other people bristle at the slightest hint of condescension. They want to be treated as an equal by the preacher, or perhaps as a little bit above him. If given a choice, they would much rather look down on him than vice versa. These people want to be "talked up to."

14. Preachers are often alarmed to discover that the people in the congregation know a lot more about "life" than does the preacher. They certainly know more about their own lives and about "the world." What they do not know is the relation of the Bible to life, theology to life, the gospel to life. That is, they do not know this in an intellectual way. They may know it subconsciously or unconsciously. Some of these people want clarification. They want the relationship between the gospel and their lives to be made clearer to them.

This is a partial listing. There are many other types of desires. If a preacher tries to please all types of people, he will say absolutely nothing that helps anyone and will certainly be dishonest with himself. If people in the congregation want a preacher who will speak words which all kinds of people want to hear, they are asking the impossible from any man of integrity. As one of the laymen in a church in our area said to one of our seminary students recently, "If you have learned that you can't and shouldn't please everyone, you have learned a lot already."

Lay Preaching

Do you have the feeling, as I often do, that preachers " miss the boat " by not including the congregation in the preaching task? So many preachers think of themselves as the only preachers in the whole congregation. There they stand — the preachers — the lonely yet noble ones, up there in the pulpit being preachers *to* and *for* the congregation. Why should they be so alone?

Try training laymen to preach. More of us in the congregation would like to share with one another. If preaching is witnessing to the congregation concerning that which we have found to be valid and meaningful in our own lives (and surely this is central to most preaching), then there must be a number of people in the congregation who could do this. As a preacher I can tell the congregation what I have found to be of significance. But how much better off all of us would be if the job were passed around. If layman after layman (and laywomen also) were to get up in the pulpit and witness to what he or she has discovered — what he or she has discovered in his reading of the Bible, in daily experiences, in living with fellow Christians or with anyone else, in his contacts with people in his job, his clubs, and his social activities. Why is the paid preacher the only one who has something to offer from the pulpit? Surely we have a mutual ministry.

Some are called to preach. But only one person in a congregation? Not everyone in the congregation can preach. But surely more could than just the paid preacher. Why not help laymen who have an interest, a concern, and some ability to learn how to preach?

Think of the effect it might have if someone other than the paid preacher, the professionally religious, the " hired Christian," were to speak of life and death. It might make the demand of the Christian gospel much more powerful. To a degree, a layman can escape the usual judgment of a preacher made by a congregation who write him off as one who gets paid for " bawling us out." Laymen don't get paid for it. Laymen might say something because they believe it. Not that we should fire all the paid preachers. But perhaps we could enable the paid preacher to be an " enabler," to be a teacher as well as a preacher. To be a teacher of ministers, an " equipper of the saints for ministry."

If it is true that the pastor is an equipper of people for ministry, then surely the ministry of some people could include preaching. We equip laymen to work on boards and committees, we equip them to serve in the community, we equip them to do visitation. Some churches equip the laymen to do pastoral care. Why not equip some of them to preach? Is preaching such a unique job that only the professional clergy can do it? I doubt it. It is obvious that it is not only the professional clergy who can administer the church, render pastoral care, visit the sick and imprisoned, and teach in the church school. Perhaps it is not so obvious, but just as valid, to say that it is not only the professional clergy who can preach. If we were willing to try, we might discover that there are many potential preachers in the congregation.

I can envision a time when a pastor would preach on two Sundays a month, a layman from the congregation would preach on another Sunday, and a guest from outside the congregation — a clergyman or a layman — would preach on the fourth Sunday. We might be more of a community of believers and workers if this would happen. We might sense our common responsibility and not palm everything off on the pastor. And we might speak to one another the words of life that we need to hear — not only from the pulpit but in many other situations.

III | The Preacher and the Preaching Event

W̲ₑ ᴛᴜʀɴ ɴᴏᴡ to the preacher. Here is the man who has to stand behind the pulpit on a Sunday morning and assume the major responsibility for making something of significance happen among a group of people, some of whom are receptive, some of whom aren't sure, and perhaps (though I doubt this) some of whom couldn't care less — an awesome responsibility. What I am concerned about in the following group of essays is that the preacher take his responsibility seriously.

I identify with this man — this preacher. I have been there. What I have to say is confessional. I am concerned about and angry with myself as a preacher. This comes out in the essays. The first essay is on "Caring" because that is at the center. Everything else I have to say follows from this. In "Forgiveness" I identify with both the preacher and the congregation. "Certainty" is a summary of a major concern of my whole ministry. Here I am really talking to myself, and I am both A and B. The essay on "Self-love" is again a dialogue with myself. "The Image" is a composite picture of some preachers I have known. I identify with them, and yet I also speak a critical word. "Communication and Caring" is based on a number of conversations with frustrated laymen and preachers.

"Concern or Despair?" is written, to some extent, in anger. I have heard so much preaching that is despairing that I felt that I needed to react to it — hopefully in a constructive way. "Humility" is intensely personal. It was written after reading some of the writings of Abraham Heschel. "Coming Up with Something" is based primarily on the experience of trying to answer seminarians who ask the questions dealt with in the essay. "Celebration" was written in response to Ross Synder's views on worship. It is autobiographical. "Ambition" is another "talking to myself" kind of dialogue. The essay on "Anger" is a reaction to a number of preachers whom I have heard over the years. The two final essays, "The Faith Crisis" and "Does It Matter?" are personal testimonies. They are at the end of the chapter because I feel the necessity of ending as I begin, with a statement of my deepest convictions. I have been harsh on preachers, but this is a part of being harsh on myself and is also a necessary path to take in order to come out with something that is more positive and constructive.

Caring

The essence of preaching is caring. Unless I care, there is no need for me to preach at all. I must look at myself and ask if I care.

All of us care about something. But a preacher cannot get by with caring about some *thing*. If I only care about things — ideas, concepts, causes — I may make a very fine writer or researcher or social reformer, but I will not be much of a preacher. If I am to be a preacher, I must care about people — not about people in general (how can you care about an abstraction such as "people in general"?), but people in the congregation I serve.

We often hear that the real test of a pastor is how he hon-

estly responds to the question, Do you love people? This is a
bit misleading. No one loves "people." When we love, we love
specific persons. Maybe God can love all people with undif-
ferentiating love. But you and I are human beings. Our loving
of people is always specific. I love Joyce and Jim and Jane,
and Jesse and Jerry. I do not love each one of them equally or
in exactly the same way, but I love them. I care about them.
Not just collectively, but as individuals. As a preacher I do not
love the congregation. I love certain people in the congregation.
There are people within the congregation with whom I have
a rather deep relationship. Hopefully, however, I care about
each of the persons in the congregation. " Love " would be
too forceful and too precious a word to use for my relationship
with all of the people in the congregation. " Caring " may get
at what I experience a little better. I care about what happens to
George, though I will never be close to him and will never
really understand him. At least I doubt if I will. Yet I care
about him. When his world begins to fall apart, I will go to
him and I will offer my help. I will think of him in the sermons I preach. I will try to find places where he can work and
grow. But I don't really love George. We don't have much of
a relationship. Yet, I care about him. Does this make sense?

When I preach, I need to *love some* of the people and *care*
about *all* of them. I mean the people in this congregation, the
people who are here this morning, even though not all of them
are members of the church. When I say " congregation," I
mean anyone who is in the sanctuary on this particular morning or evening, whether a member of the church or not. I care
about all of them. Not because they are lovely people, though
most of them are lovelier than I would give them credit for
being. Not because I like them. I genuinely like only about one
half to three fourths of the congregation. This is probably mutual. I am antagonistic to a fair number of the people. This is

probably mutual also. It depends on whether or not as a congregation we have allowed ourselves to deal with controversy. If we have, then most of us are somewhat aware of our antagonisms and hostility toward each other. This is good. But I find myself caring about the man who is blocking all our efforts to do progressive work in the board of deacons. Not because I like him, but because he too needs to become human. He needs to come out of his prison, and it may be that he will find a way out through our church fellowship. Particularly if we stay with him.

What do I think of as I sit in the pulpit chair on a Sunday morning? I think of Phil. The sermon this morning is about the need for honesty in human relationships. Phil is in selling. He finds it very difficult to be wholly honest in his relationships. He has to say what will sell the product, and he cannot tell the whole truth to a potential customer. He has to appear to be convinced that this product is needed by the consumer, even though he is not convinced. I need to think of Phil as I preach this sermon, and to keep myself from doing the easy thing — tearing into dishonesty in a vicious, judgmental, self-righteous way, laying down the law, acting as if I know God's will. God has a will for Phil too. It may include his honesty *and* his dishonesty. Perhaps Phil needs to be the best salesman he can be. In time he may move up the ladder in his company and get into a policy-making post which will enable him to confront the other salesmen with what honesty means in their business. But he will not be of much help to them if he fails to struggle with this problem right now. I need to support Phil in this struggle, not take the easy way out and just make him feel guiltier. Nor, for that matter, can I let him " get off the hook " by his saying, " This guy just doesn't understand my job — I can't follow this idealistic standard in my work."

I must look at myself and ask if I care.

Forgiveness

It is so terribly easy to be moralistic, isn't it? We look at the congregation and we feel that what is missing is *commitment* — their commitment. If only the people were more committed. Then they would come to church more often. Then they would serve on the boards and committees without complaining. They would respond to calls for service in the community. So we preach about commitment. But somehow our preaching sounds so moralistic.

We keep berating the people. " Jesus went all the way for our salvation. He did not turn away from the cross." Are we asking people, over and over again, to take up their crosses? But what are the results? More commitment? I doubt it. More guilt, perhaps. I often think that about all that a lot of our preaching about commitment produces is more useless guilt. Some people, usually those who are actively involved in the church already, feel guilty about not being more committed. Those people who are not actively involved feel vaguely guilty and resolve halfheartedly to do something about it — but they don't. Or they write off what the minister says as " preacher talk." And that is actually what it is — preacher talk. We are paid to shape up the troops, shout them into line. But these people are not troops. They don't shape up. They don't fall into line. And why should they?

Don't we often berate people for their lack of commitment because we do not believe, deep down within our souls, that we are forgiven? We don't believe that we are accepted by God and by others as fallible, essentially ordinary human beings. We have never accepted forgiveness for being human. We lack pride in our humanity. We wish we were gods. But we aren't, and we feel guilty.

Isn't it rather fruitless to feel guilty because we are not bearing crosses? to feel guilty because you and I are not Jesus? We make Jesus so noble, so divine, as if he set his face like a flint and went forward into the fray — God's warrior. Such noble commitment. I don't set my face like a flint. So I am a bad boy. Such romantic nonsense. Jesus said, " If it be possible, let this cup pass from me." Remember him saying, " My God, my God, why hast thou forsaken me? " Jesus was no romantic. He did not make Cyrano-like speeches, full of bravado, either genuine or false.

" Neither do I condemn you." " Your sins are forgiven. Go in peace." Forgiven. Forgiven for being human. For being nothing but a man. How glorious to be nothing but a man. How wonderful! I don't have to be God. I am not condemned for being human. I am forgiven. This is wild, weird — I don't understand it. You mean I don't have to prove myself to God or to other people? I can actually be me? Being me is worth something? Me, with my lack of commitment, my mistakes, my unwillingness to risk? Me?

Of course the congregation is not committed. To what are we to be committed? What makes us so sure as pastors that coming to church indicates a significant commitment? Are we so certain that being on boards and committees shows a real commitment to what is important? Can we know for sure that service in the community is all that meaningful and significant? We don't know that much. We are not God. We don't know what we need to ask people to do to show their commitment. Why can't we be more humble about our knowledge and our lack of knowledge?

To this the pastor may reply: " Look, Frank, I know you're a busy man. But you know, there is a need for someone who can get some men together in our church and meet with them one night a week for three weeks and help them see what it means to be a Christian in their jobs. You are wrestling with this matter yourself, as I know from our talks together. I think you could help these guys. What do you think? Do you think it might be exciting? Do you think it would be worth doing? Frankly, I don't know if it would or not, but I would like for you to give it a try."

Commitment? Why don't we respect a person enough to ask him what he thinks is worth giving himself to? Why do we berate him and tell him "Do this, do that," without ever asking for his counsel? Real commitment is not something I can force on someone. Real commitment is something a person chooses freely. How about letting up on the laymen? How about treating them as we want to be treated — as human, glad to be human, able to make up our own minds, forgiven sinners.

I cannot condemn you. How could I? I am human too.

Certainty

A: Do I always have to believe 100 percent in what I am saying? How can I be completely honest?

B: Well, you wouldn't say something from the pulpit that you didn't believe, would you?

A: I wouldn't get up there and intentionally lie, no. But I say things of which I am not absolutely certain.

B: Oh, sure, I do that too. But, after all, I'm not God.

A: Yes, but if we're to speak God's word to the people, don't we have to be certain about what we are saying? Certain that it is God's word? It is a tremendous responsibility, getting up there and preaching.

B: But how can you be certain? Let's say you are talking about sin, O.K.? And you say that adultery is sin. Now there's a good basis for saying that in the Bible. But aren't there circumstances where adultery might be the most human and humane thing to do?

A: That's a pretty " far out " illustration. I can't think of any instance where adultery would be a humane thing to do. How about something like my preaching about sin, and I say that you should always be honest in your business? But I know that a salesman often has to tell a prospective customer that his product is better than he knows it really is. If he doesn't do this, he won't draw his money, and if he doesn't do that, he won't be able to support his children.

B: O.K. Perhaps your illustration is better. Though the adultery thing kind of intrigues me. The point in either illustration is that you have some rules from the Bible, but it is hard to apply them literally in a real-life situation.

A: For that matter, can you be certain about the validity of something merely because it is in the Bible? Let's say that you preached strictly from the Bible, sort of just repeating what it says and that is that. Would you then be completely credible? Would you be speaking out of certainty or with divine authority?

B: I would say no. You wouldn't be, and for a number of reasons. First, the Bible is written by men, not God, and men are human and fallible. Second, God doesn't reveal words, statements, written truths. He reveals himself, his presence. He reveals us to each other. His will is not spelled out neatly in words. Third, why create human beings if they are just passive receptacles for truths? Don't people have to develop truths, create valid living? After all, we are free. God created us free.

A: But God didn't give us license to believe anything we want to, say anything we want to and pass it off as the truth.

B: But my point is that truth is not a statement, a series of words that are " the right words." Truth is like an attitude, or a way of living my life. If I live my life in a continuous attempt to give myself to other people, to receive from them, to co-operate with them in actions that matter, to be human and humane to my fellow creatures, then I am trying to live the truth.

A: Very nice. Very noble. But you aren't staying away from words. I can say from the pulpit, "Live your life in a continuous attempt to give yourself to other people, et cetera, et cetera," and I am mouthing a true statement in your way of looking at it. Or maybe if I said, " God wants you to live your life in a continuous attempt, and so forth." That's a statement, and it is either true or it is false.

B: It isn't true or false as a statement. It depends on whether or not it adequately reflects what you know to be true from experience.

A: I'm getting confused. I started out with asking whether or not I have to believe with certainty what I say from the pulpit. I still don't have the answer to that one.

B: All right, " nonphilosopher," let's start again. You and I can't be certain that we are saying from the pulpit exactly what God wants us to say. Right?

A: I am *certainly* not certain that I am saying from the pulpit what God wants me to say — I think.

B: You're hedging.

A: O.K. I don't feel as if I am saying God's words after him when I speak from the pulpit. How's that?

B: I'm willing to " jump off " from there.

A: Thank you, kind sir.

B: You are welcome — with feeling. Anyway, what you need to do, what I need to do too, is to speak a word — hopefully more than one word — of helpfulness to the people in the congregation. They are there to hear something that will help them live better. The best I can do is to speak out of my knowledge of the Bible, the history of the church, indeed, the history of mankind as I know it, and out of my own experience and the experiences of those around me — including the experiences of the congregation to whom I speak. I speak as one Christian to others — out of our common experience and knowledge, with the insight derived from the studies I have mentioned. That is all I can do. And I can hope that, God willing, I am helping them. Or we are helping each other — helping each other in a way that we need to be helped. In a way that God wants us to be helped. But I can't be certain of this — certain that we are helping each other. We can never be certain, but it is worth the risk.

A: I suppose it is. It better be, because that is the way it is. But it is an awfully uncertain task.

B: Yes, and we should be grateful rather than sorry that we aren't God.

A: How do you mean?

B: I said that we should be thankful we aren't God.

A: Why?

B: Because I would imagine that being God would be pretty rough. You would always have to be right. Since we are human beings, we don't always have to be right. Not only that, but we can help our fellow human beings more when we realize that we do not have to be right all the time. Then we identify with each other more and we work together in a common quest.

A: You mean that I should realize that I do not have to worry about being right all the time. After all, I am not God. I just have to worry about being a human being who is willing to share with other human beings on the same level and with the realization that we are all in this thing together. Is that what you mean?

B: Something like that.

Self-love

The best preachers are those who love themselves. If you love yourself, you accept yourself, you like yourself, you forgive yourself, you enjoy being yourself, you have decided that you are of worth.

As a child, I used to be by myself quite a bit. I would spin daydreams. I would play intricate games in my own mind. Characters would be created in my imagination, and I would be a part of all of these characters, for they were all caricatures of bits and pieces of my own personality. These characters would take their places in the play, and they would walk and speak and play interesting roles. They fascinated me, for they were telling me about myself. I learned to enjoy being by myself. I interested me. And thus what happened, I suppose, was that I came to judge myself as being of worth.

A: Isn't it selfish to love yourself?

B: But the love that you have for yourself is the most unselfish love there is.

A: Unselfish — how do you mean?

B: I mean that if you love yourself you accept yourself as you are. You do not demand that you meet a certain standard in order to be loved. You totally affirm your own being. You say, " This is me, and I am glad."

A: But what about other people? Shouldn't most of your love be directed toward other people?

B: You will find it very difficult to love other people if you do not love yourself. Instead, you will be wanting them to give you something that only you can give yourself. You will be wanting them to tell you, to prove to you, that you are of worth. This is too much to demand of another person. It isn't fair. And, anyway, even if another person did tell you that you are worth something to him, this would not satisfy you. *You* have to believe that you are of worth. You have to love yourself. Otherwise, you will use other people. When you believe with all your heart, when you love yourself with all your heart, then you are free to truly love other people and not to *use* them.

A: This may be, but you have said nothing about God. Doesn't he have anything to do with all this?

B: Like what?

A: Like aren't you supposed to love God more than anyone? And doesn't he have to love you for you to really love yourself?

B: I am not sure that I love God. I think " grateful " might be a better term. I am grateful to him — grateful that he loves me, that he forgives me, that he accepts me. Somehow this helps me to love myself. It is like I am saying " Amen " to myself or saying " Amen " to God's estimate of me. God says to me " You are of worth." I say " Amen." And I say it gratefully. I don't love him in that I forgive him or accept him or say that he is of worth. He does that for me, but I can't do that for him. I am not his God.

If you are to preach, you need to believe that you have something to give. Otherwise, why take up the time of the congregation? And not only that you have something to give, but you have something *unique* to give. It takes a great deal of self-love to believe this. There is no one like you in the whole world. God has made you one of a kind. You have something unique to give to people. Not a unique idea — but the giving of an idea in a unique way. Not unique words — you use the same language everyone uses — but words said by *you,* and you are one of a kind. What you have to give that is unique is yourself. Or, more theologically, God's giving of himself through your uniqueness. Through you, because of you, often in spite of or over against you, but you are there in that pulpit and no one else is there. That is you there. There has never been a time in history like this time. There will never be again. Something can happen at this time and in this place that can never happen again in all eternity. You can give yourself to these people in your unique way. You can be open to God's giving of himself through you in this place, at this time, in a unique moment.

The Image

It is hard to respect yourself when you know that you are playing a game with the congregation. Here is an image: Preacher. Perhaps a preacher I have known in my past. Perhaps a preacher in the same town whom everyone looks up to. Perhaps a famous preacher. Perhaps a figment of my imagination — an idealization. Here is an image: Preacher. I am trying to fit that image. When I ascend to the pulpit, I act out that part. Not very well. Not with as much finesse as I would wish. But I act the part. I play a game. I play a role.

I am a preacher. I am in front of these people. Now I am called by God to be here. I am God's man. His mouthpiece. I am to speak for him — like Reverend Johnson used to. Now there was a man. Tall in the pulpit. Commanding. The people listened to him. He stood erect like this and spoke in a deep, resonant voice. The people should respect me and what I have to say. After all, I speak God's word. Like Reverend Johnson used to. There was a man.

After thirty years, what have you done?

You have said the words and baptized the children and visited the sick.
And what have you done?
Who are you?
Have you ever been who you are?
Has it ever been you who stood in that pulpit?

Has it ever been you at that bedside in the hospital room?
Has it ever been you in bed with your wife?

*Or has it always been someone else: the pastor, the preacher,
the fine young man, the steady and stable middle-aged parson,
the elderly gentleman — a kindly man.*

Has it ever been you?

Has God ever spoken through you, or has he wasted his
breath by trying to breathe life into an image, an icon, a plaster
figure?

Communication and Caring

Perhaps " preacher " is not a good title for him. " Communicator " might be a better name. A preacher is one who communicates with people. He is a communicative person. What
does it mean to be a communicative person?

A: What do you think of Reverend Stout's preaching?

B: Well, he is a nice guy.

A: Yes, but what do you think of his preaching?

B: I don't listen too closely really. Sermons never do much
for me.

A: I've heard sermons that did something for me, but his
sure don't.

B: Yeah, I guess you're right. They don't do anything for
me either.

A: You know what I think?

B: What?

A: I think he's scared.

B: Scared? He doesn't look frightened to me.

A: No, I mean, I think he is scared of us — of the people
in the congregation.

B: What makes you think so?

A: Well, he stands up there behind the pulpit and hides from us. He talks to himself. That is what he is really doing. He is talking to himself. And he very seldom looks at us, and when he does, he looks away immediately. The other Sunday — I guess it was last Sunday, as a matter of fact — I decided to test him out, so I looked directly at him all through his sermon, and whenever he happened to look at me, he turned his head immediately. I think he was scared to look at me square in the face.

B: You aren't that handsome, you know.

A: You know what I mean.

B: Maybe you're right. I have noticed that he seems preoccupied when he is up there in the pulpit. He wants to get through what he is doing and get home for dinner probably — like most of us.

A: But he is this way in other places too. My mother-in-law passed away a while back and he came to our house and talked with my wife and me. And I felt like this was a duty for him — something he knew he was supposed to do but didn't really want to. He said all the right things, but he didn't really care. My wife said the same thing. She didn't feel comforted at all.

B: I don't like to speak against the preacher, but I remember a few months ago when he was giving a talk to our Boy Scout troop. He was talking about how it is rough to be a kid these days and how there are a lot of temptations to drink and smoke and fool around and stuff like that, and the kids could care less — you know. Anyway, after the talk was over, he had to leave right away to get to another meeting he said. But I happen to know that he had a golf date with the Catholic priest. Not that the kids wanted him to stick around anyway. But like you say, maybe he is scared and is running away.

If I were to put a definition of communication into one concise sentence, I would say, "Communication is caring." If you care about something, you will communicate it. If you care about someone, you will communicate with him. This doesn't mean that you will communicate effectively. But it does mean that you will try to do so, and you will learn how to do better — if you really care. But it is difficult to really care. This requires everything of us, more than many of us are willing to give.

Let us look in on a session between Reverend Stout and his Catholic-priest friend.

Stout: You know, Jack, you're about the only one I can talk to. I'm at my wit's end.

Priest: What's going on, Fred?

S.: I'm not quite sure. I mean I'm not quite sure what is really going on. I know what the symptoms are, but I haven't gotten at the cause yet. Maybe I am afraid to.

P.: What are the symptoms?

S.: I just don't have my heart in it anymore. I go through the motions. I do all the things you're supposed to do: preach, visit, run things, go to meetings, get active in the community — all the right things. But my heart isn't in it anymore. I am just going through the motions.

P.: Maybe you're tired and you need a vacation.

S.: No, I had a vacation three or four months ago. It isn't that. I just, I just don't seem to have the mental or moral or something energy to "get with it." Do you know that I watch an average of four hours of TV a day? And even more on Saturday and Sunday. I can't drive myself into my work anymore. I just want to get away from it and away from myself. I'm scared, Jack. I'm afraid I've lost the spirit or the call or whatever it is. I don't care about people anymore. I am not sure I even care about myself.

It can be terribly devastating for a pastor to discover that he doesn't care about people. He is uncommunicative because he does not want to communicate. He is afraid to communicate. He is afraid of people and afraid that they will find out that he doesn't care about them. We cannot go into the matter of why he doesn't care. This is not a book on psychotherapy. But I do feel that the point is valid that at the root of communication is caring, and the basic cause of noncommunication is not caring. To put it simply again: If I care about you, I will try by every means in my power to communicate with you. If I do not care about you, I will either leave you alone or run from you.

Concern or Despair?

"Who you are speaks louder than what you say." Or is this more accurate: "Who you are *is* what you say"? One of the most influential writers in the field of communication is Marshall McLuhan. His famous dictum, "The medium is the message," is familiar to many of us. Though such a phrase can be used badly, I think it has something to say to us about preaching. I have heard people speak about love with hate in their voices. They speak of love hatefully. What they say is about love, who they are are people who are hating. What comes through to the audience is hate, not love. Thus what they *say* (communicate) to the audience is hate, not words about love. "Who you are *is* what you say." The medium of who you are is the message that gets through to people.

If I say to you, "I care about you," and I say it in a way that "says" to you, "How could you be so stupid as to not realize that I care about you — now get this through your thick skull," then you know that the word "care" is being used by me in an uncaring manner. I don't care about you at all. I care about getting something through to you whether you like it or not. I care about beating you over the head with an idea that I want you to grasp. I want to get rid of having to worry about how you feel about me. Actually, I only care about myself. I want you to quit demanding something of me — such as real caring.

In our day, it is interesting how often we confuse *concern* with *despair*. A preacher may think that he is concerned about the local congregation of which he is the pastor. He expresses his concern from the pulpit, he expresses it in meetings, he expresses it to individuals. But he does not really communicate concern. He communicates despair. You have all heard the preacher who says something like this from the pulpit:

" I want to lay a concern on your hearts. I am afraid that this church is going downhill. We are not getting the number of people out on a Sunday morning that we used to. Our Sunday school is dwindling. Hardly anyone comes out to Wednesday evening services anymore. But even more important, what are we actually doing in this community that amounts to anything? What are we doing for people? Oh, we do a little bit now and then, particularly on Thanksgiving and Christmas, but very little. I am concerned about this and I want all of us to look at the situation very carefully and prayerfully."

What is communicated here? Concern or despair? Perhaps if I paint the picture for you a little more graphically and say that the preacher has delivered himself of this message with a tense gripping of the pulpit, a furrowed brow, and a generally agitated manner, then you will see more fully what he has communicated. He is *so* concerned. But the people sit in the congregation and many of them are thinking: " I wonder if some other church could use more people and if something is going on there that is exciting? I sure don't want to be part of a dying enterprise. If he is discouraged, how can we do anything? I think I'll go to another church next Sunday and see how they are doing."

As preachers we often say more to the congregation about what we really feel, what is really motivating us, than we realize. It is difficult to fool a congregation. Most of us are not adept enough to disguise our true feelings. We communicate how we feel — how we actually feel. And people are not fooled.

What does a person want from a preacher? One of the basic needs we have as people is to hear from a person who knows what it is to live a significant life. We want to hear from a person who has found out how to live fully, vibrantly, and honestly. When we hear from such a person, we rejoice that we are human, that we can become someone, that all is not lost. We need desperately to know that human life can be a glorious thing, that authentic existence is possible. We need living water from a well that does not run dry. We can't get this from another human being, but we can be helped toward finding it from another human being. Preaching is one man telling other men of the food that needs to be eaten and of how they can come and get in on this banquet. We are inviting people to a banquet, not to a wake.

Humility

It takes a lot of gall to get up to preach. I am assuming that I have something to say. Not just something — something significant, something that will illumine men's lives, something that will draw the veil from the mystery.

I am not good at drawing veils. I do not understand life. I do not even understand what I think I know. There is so much mystery in this world, how can we ever presume to say anything that makes sense? It is as if I pick up a pebble from a beach and say: "This is it. This is the key. Once we understand this pebble we will understand the beach and the land

and the ocean." But this pebble looks like the others. And even this pebble, this one infinitesimal pebble, is so complex that I cannot begin to understand it or even understand why it is possible for me to pick up a pebble or even think about one.

I exhibit such presumption in speaking about God. I do not even understand myself, let alone God. I don't know what to say to my wife that lets her know I love her, let alone say something about God that frees people to live. In the midst of mystery, I often think the best response is to stand mute. To stand behind the pulpit and keep silent. Drink in the wonder of life and be silent. I say a word and immediately I know it is not valid. Qualifications are used such as, "Well, I don't mean that exactly " or, "Maybe we should look at it this way." Circumlocutions — roads that looked nice and led to dead ends.

Walking into a pulpit is like walking into a dark wood. I see the trees, but they all look alike. There are paths between them, but the paths lead only to more trees and more paths. The light is very faint. I hear the rustling of leaves or brush or something and I wonder if it is all wind or if others are there with me. I could get lost in this wood and never find my way out. The stars are hidden beyond the impenetrable foliage. I do not understand these woods. They say that these are the Woods of God. But that doesn't help very much. The woods are still frightening and impenetrable.

How do we deal with mystery?

Perhaps we wait for revelation. But revelation is not the dispelling of mystery. Revelation helps. It helps us to deal a bit with the mystery. It helps us to see what can be done — in a way. In the face of mystery, it is good to know that we are to love. But what is love? How is it done? Can we express love and have the other know it is love? And all our own receiving, our own taking of love seems not of one piece but of many. Seems not one event, but a cluster of happenings, joys,

fears, and wonder. In the midst of mystery, we receive a revelation. The only way to live in God's Woods is to grasp the
hand of our brothers. This is good. This is valid. It is worth
saying. But it doesn't take us out of the woods. This is the next
point of revelation — you will never get out of the woods.

As I ascend this pulpit and look at these people I ask for
help. I ask that all of us will be given the grace to cry " Help! "
That all of us, each one utterly unique, may learn to live with
the mystery of life, not happily as if we cared no more for it,
but with the understanding that it is mystery with which we
live, not knowledge, that I can only reach out, not find, that
we can only hope and pray and chance the act that may drop
us into darkness or shoot us up into light.

How can a preacher possibly stand in front of a congregation and say honestly to himself, " I know what all of you
need to hear "? Even Jesus tried parables, Old Testament quo-
tations, healings, acts of courage, and they crucified him. Did
he know what we needed to hear? He tried to say what needed
to be said, but we poor men and women listen with ears that
often do not hear and hear only what we want to hear, and
even at best the words, even the words of Jesus, are garbled,
mumbled — pitifully poor efforts to penetrate the mystery.

I do not know what you need to hear. I can only guess, make
stabs in the dark, grasp your hand, and ask you to help me
too. I stand here as one other person in the dark woods and tell
you, with trembling, with conviction, with hope, that these are
the Woods of God. Does that help? What are you hearing in
the rustling leaves and the crackling sticks?

Coming Up with Something

" How in heaven's name can you possibly come up with a
winner every Sunday? I would be lucky to be able to work up

one decent sermon a month."

" It is brutal to ask a man to say something every Sunday, often twice on Sunday, that is really significant, that says anything worth saying. It is too much to ask."

" I give up. It can't be done. I just have to use another man's sermon outlines or dip into *The Interpreter's Bible* again. I can't come up with something fresh and relevant every single week."

I wonder if these complaints appear to be something that they are not? It looks as if the men making these complaints are concerned with saying something relevant and significant every single Sunday. They correctly understand that it is very difficult to do so. It would appear that they are focusing on the problem of content — what can be said that is important. But is this their real concern? Is it possible that they are more concerned with their own image? That is, how they will look to their congregations each Sunday. Will the congregations greet them with open arms or will they sit and yawn and say to themselves, " Well, maybe next week " or, " Here we go again, another exercise in trivia." Are these pastors concerned more with how they look, how they are accepted or rejected by the congregation, than whether or not they are saying anything worth saying?

A: Boy, that sermon went over great last Sunday!

B: What was the sermon about?

A: Oh, it was about love of neighbor.

B: What did you say?

A: Something about the need for really giving of yourself. But it was the illustration about that family in Appalachia that really got to them. They will never forget it. Everyone commented on it.

B: What did the illustration illustrate?

A: Oh, you know, how even in difficult situations the love

of neighbor can be shown.

B: A really significant sermon, eh?

A: It really wowed 'em!

We hear the preparation for a sermon referred to as "priming the pump." You try to find a little water that will get the pump started and then you pump away — hopefully with ease and assurance. On Wednesday or Thursday we try to prime the pump. Read something that will stimulate our thinking, see a movie or a television show, maybe go to a conference, or conduct a counseling session. Something that will prime the pump, get things in motion, start the ball rolling, start the wheels turning. It will soon be Sunday, and we will be "onstage" again. We have to find a script.

> There will be time, there will be time
> To prepare a face to meet the faces
>   that you meet.
> (T. S. Eliot, *The Complete Poems and Plays*, p. 4;
>   Harcourt, Brace & Co., Inc., 1952.)

Isn't this what we are doing? Not preparing a sermon, a message, but preparing a face to meet the faces that we meet. So that we won't be laughed at, unless we tell a joke, so that we won't be thought ill of, so that we will be accepted and loved and looked up to. How do you come up "preacher" every Sunday? How do you make a good impression every Sunday? How can you "come across" every Sunday? Is this our question?

It is not a very important question, is it? Oh, yes, if you were a television performer, it would be an important question. If you had to "go on," to be "onstage" every week, it would be an important question. But you are a preacher, a minister, a communicator of the gospel.

My reflection was smiling in the mirror, but it seemed to me that my smile was double. . . . It seemed to me that every one I encountered was looking at me with a hidden smile. I even had the impression, at that time, that people were tripping me up. Two or three times, in fact, I stumbled as I entered public places. Once, even, I went sprawling on the floor. (Albert Camus, *The Fall*, pp. 40, 78; Vintage Books, Inc., 1956.)

Whose face am I preparing to meet? The faces of others? No, my own face. For it is ultimately myself with whom I have to do. Preparing the face to meet other faces is an escape from seeing my own face. Am I prepared to meet myself on Sunday morning? Some preachers have a sign on the back of their pulpits that only they can read. The sign says, " Sir, we would see Jesus." I wonder what would happen if the sign read, " Sir, we would see *you.*" Perhaps you are the last person you want to see.

The point is not to "make a hit," to "score a success," to " go over great." The point is to say something that matters — that matters to you and that can matter to those who hear you. The point is to preach the gospel, the gospel of the man who mattered. The man who did not go "onstage" when he got up to preach, but who said what he knew to be true, who said it with his life and his dying, with his crying and his laughing, with his joy and his despair. The man who never looked at mirrors, but looked through his own eyes — his eyes — at the world of his Father. He looked with compassion — *his* compassion — not a borrowed compassion. Not a prepared compassion. Not a love that was rehearsed and polished. A love that was who he was and why he was.

Let us grant that the hidden motive behind the desire to come up with something fresh each Sunday can be a desire to perform, to "go over big," and thus to escape an encounter with ourselves and with what matters. But the question remains, does it not? How do you come up with something significant in terms of sermon content each Sunday?

It seems to me that there are certain ways of " coming up with something " that are bad ways. Going through a book of sermon starters, for example. Looking at someone else's sermons, for example. What is the context in which *you* preach? It isn't the same context as that in which the man preached who wrote the sermon-starter book, nor is it the same context in which Fosdick or Thielicke or Barth lived.

Jesus announced that the Kingdom of God was among the people of first-century Palestine. It was among, with, in, between, them. And so it is in our time. The job of the preacher is to show the people of a given congregation where the Kingdom of God is " breaking out," being realized, being fought against, in their midst. You and I will never be able to preach anything that is significant unless we attempt to discover how and where the Kingdom of God is becoming known in the community in which we minister.

The sensitive preacher is one who is sensitive to his community. He is so sensitive that he rejoices with those who celebrate the joys of the community and weeps with those who weep for this Jerusalem. It is out of his joy and his weeping that he preaches. It is out of his reading of the Bible and other works, his knowing of the church's struggle through the centuries, his participation in the theological discussions of his time, that he gains perspective on the laughing and the weeping of his community. If the preacher is sensitive, he cannot help speaking. He needs perspective on what is happening. And he needs to share this perspective with others and learn from their perspectives.

The problem is not to come up with something significant every Sunday. The problem is to rule out a whole host of problems and come up with what is crucial *for this particular time*.

It is like the doctor who has to rule out a whole group of diseases in order to come up with what he thinks may be the problem.

It is not a matter of coming up with a lively topic to be discussed, a lecture on something interesting. It is a matter of ruling out a lot of possibilities and focusing on what is crucial *this* week, *this* Sunday, *this* moment in the history of *this* community. What is happening in our town that needs the perspective of the Bible and of the history of the church in order that we may understand its meaning? Which event in our town, which problem in our lives, which joy, which sorrow, which cause for celebration, which cause for grief, must I deal with this Sunday? Not what can I *include,* but what can I afford to *exclude?* What is the crucial point, the place at which the Kingdom of God is breaking in now? Would that I could preach five sermons this Sunday in order to try to give some perspective to the gamut of problems and events that call out for interpretation.

If you have nothing to say this Sunday, you are either insensitive to your community, or you are enslaved to a " snappy topic " rationale for preaching, or you feel honestly, deep in your own heart, that silence is the best response to the agony of your community.

Celebration

Tomorrow morning when I get up in front of the people, I will celebrate. I will say, " These things are happening and I must celebrate them." And then I will list those events which I wish to celebrate. Perhaps after each item we could all repeat some kind of refrain such as, " He came that we may have life " or, " Lord, we thank thee for thy gifts." Then after I list those things which I want to celebrate, perhaps others in the congregation could speak of what they wish to celebrate. Isn't this preaching? Isn't this speaking of the gospel in a very direct way, a specific way? I think so.

What shall I celebrate? I shall celebrate George's decision to run for the school board. He had to quit the chairmanship of the deacons in order to do it. I think I shall celebrate this. I shall celebrate Hazel and Frank's new baby. They didn't think they could ever have children. They had waited so long. Another cause for celebration: St. Agnes R. C. Church is getting a new priest. He is young and liberal, I hear. I look forward to working with him. I will celebrate the grant our Community Action Program received from the Government. Now we can build those swimming pools, and hire those recreation leaders. And I can celebrate Jack's election to a top job in the union where he works. Dennis' engagement to Joyce. The death of Fred's grandmother, who had hung on for so long. Perhaps I had better not list too many causes for celebration. The congregation will want to celebrate also. Will they see the difference between this and " Count your blessings, name them one by one "? Because that was usually some very individual kind of thing. Some thing that had little to do with the community as such or even the congregation. I think that if we look at the community and the congregation and individuals, we cannot run out of events to celebrate.

Where is the judgment in this? My celebrating doesn't seem to be a prophetic type of sermon. Of course, I can't do everything in one sermon. Perhaps I am not too prophetic a person. I am really more interested in pointing out what is happening that is exciting and significant and that people should get involved in than I am in drawing attention to what is wrong and to what we should feel guilty about. Take poverty, for example. Instead of making us feel guiltier and guiltier about our affluence in the midst of poverty — and most of this guilt feeling is phony anyway — why don't we celebrate what **is** happening as we deal with poverty? Challenge the people to support the Community Action Program. People in poverty situations don't want affluent people to feel guilty. They want action. Stimulus to action. Opportunity for action. Like race relations, for example. Instead of hollering about how we don't have any Negroes in our congregation, why not talk about groups in the community that include both Negroes and whites and urge people to join these groups? and hold some of the group meetings in our church building? or, even better, in the homes of our members? Celebrate these possibilities. Or celebrate the times when Negroes have sensed their identity and have risen up against white exploitation. Celebrate these times. Wouldn't this help to sensitize the congregation to what is happening that is important?

I guess that celebrating and feeling happy, though connected, are not the same thing. I can celebrate what is happening that is great and hopeful, but I am not unqualifiedly happy about it. I can celebrate the strides we are making in race relations but be unhappy about the long road we have yet to travel. Or I can celebrate the death of Fred's grandmother, for it was a release from pain, but I cannot be happy about the fact of death and the possibility that if his grandmother had lived without this illness, she might have done a great deal more. Celebration is often a lot like observing Hanukkah in the Warsaw ghetto during World War II.

Ambition

A: So Joe got the big pulpit. Well, he has the ability, I guess.

B: I hear he's a dynamic preacher. At least his people think so. So I hear, anyway.

A: Some guys get 'em and some don't. Naturally, I am content to stay right where I am — right here in Mediocreville.

B: Oh, yes, we have a mission to the pigs and cows right where we are. A real challenge.

A: He's quite a preacher, huh?

B: That's what they say.

A: What do they mean "quite a preacher"?

B: He's popular, you know.

A: Draws the crowds, I suppose?

B: Something like that.

A: I could probably become more popular. Give 'em what they want. Jazz it up a little. Something of the Billy Graham touch — you know.

B: Somehow I don't think of you when I think of Billy Graham.

A: How often do you think of Billy Graham, you lousy liberal?

B: When I need a "straw man" to fight against.

A: I'm not thinking of Graham's theology. I'm thinking of his style. Clear, simple, to the point. Socko! Right in there! Give it to 'em straight!

B: Wouldn't you rather be truthful and a failure?

A: Truthful, maybe; failure, no. I can be truthful. I just don't say *everything* I am thinking. Say the truth, but don't make it too hard to take. Then throw in a couple of clever illustrations, speak with conviction, drive to the finish, and wind it all up with a quotation or poem that sends them out to do battle. You see, I could be popular too. Right?

B: Wrong.

A: Why wrong?

B: Because you, old buddy, are always you and not someone else. You couldn't fake it. You are too honest.

A: How do you know? Maybe there is a side of me you haven't seen yet. That I haven't even seen. I used to do some

debating in college. I could argue both sides of a question im-
partially. And I could sound convincing too. I have just as
much trickery and deceit in me as the next guy.

B: You couldn't carry it off. You would betray yourself in
the pastoral relationships. It isn't too hard to lie from the pulpit, but it is hard when you are faced with a rough counseling
session or when someone in the congregation confronts you
with a rough question or a real challenge.

A: You're probably right. I couldn't carry it off. I would
like to be a better preacher, though. Not Riverside Church,
you understand, but maybe something in suburban Cleveland.

B: Why? So you can prove something to yourself? So you
can prove that you have it?

A: Ooooh, that hurts. You've had too much of this clinical
training stuff. Already you are psychoanalyzing. O.K. I'll play
along. Because I want to prove something to myself. Because
I want to know if I have what it takes. Because I want recognition. Because I don't fully believe in myself. How's that?

B: Not a bad start. Would you like fifteen more minutes?

A: And my next point, friends, is that I am sick to death
of hacking it out here day after day, week after week, in Po-
dunk Hollow. Sick, do you hear me, sick, sick, sick. I want to
move up. Cheers and applause.

B: Why do you want to move up?

A: Quote: To prove to myself that I can do it. And because
I would have more influence. Unquote.

B: You could exert more power.

A: Now I'm power hungry?

B: Who isn't?

A: All right. I'll buy that. Prove myself to myself plus a desire for power. Anything else?

B: Yes. Why did you choose the ministry?

A: Why, I was called by God, of course.

B: Of course. Why did you choose the ministry?

A: I wanted to help people.

B: Help people do what?

A: Help people love each other more and help them find a sense of purpose and meaning in their lives.

B: You can't do that where you are?

A: Oh, sure. But there aren't very many people here.

B: Have you helped these people love each other more? Are they all loving each other now? And are they all purposeful people living meaningful lives?

A: Not all of them. Some of them — to a degree.

B: More each year perhaps?

A: I hope so.

B: Why do you want a bigger church?

A: So I can help more people.

B: Why don't you practice polygamy so that you can love more women?

A: Brother, I haven't begun to love the one I have as deeply as I should.

B: How about that?

Anger

If a man is angry, it is healthy for him to vent his anger — to explode, to blow up, to spew out his anger like lava from a volcano. Some men blow up in their living room, or to their wives, or as they weed the garden, or as they pound nails in a do-it-yourself project. Then there are preachers who do it from the pulpit. What about anger in the pulpit?

1. Misdirected anger:

Example — " I say we have to decide right here, right now, whether we are going to let the fundamentalists push us around or not. We need to stand up for what we believe. No pussyfooting around. No more delay. Will you and I stand up and be counted for Jesus Christ? Will we stand up for all that is progressive, true, just, liberal, significant? We cannot wait any longer. The issue is clear. We must take a stand right here, right now! "

It appears on the surface as if the issue is fundamentalism vs. liberalism. But the congregation knows that the preacher is raising a false issue. No one is forcing the congregation to make any decision. For some reason the preacher is raising the issue. Why? The reason, which perhaps only a few of the " ingroup " parishioners understand, is that the preacher feels that he is under attack by two or three in his own congregation. Not for any theological reason. But because of a more personal issue — he did not call on the wife of a powerful person in the congregation when she was in the hospital for a couple of days. The preacher feels himself to be under attack. He is unable to deal with this attack directly, so he vents his frustration, defensiveness, and anger by attacking a straw man. His anger is misdirected.

The trouble with this kind of anger is that it is misleading, dishonest, and nonconstructive. It is misleading because it raises issues (fundamentalist vs. liberal) which are not real issues and which will only divert energies away from important issues. It is dishonest because it is not the real issue. It is nonconstructive because the real issue is not dealt with by anyone. The preacher needs to face himself. What is really bothering him? Perhaps it is not only the attack by a certain few. It may also be the sense of guilt that he carries because he doesn't think he is a good pastor. He has a low self-image. The preacher, it seems to me, has no right to exhibit such misdirected anger. He is not playing fair with the congregation. He is refusing to face up to what is really bothering him. He is using the congregation to help him vent his anger, but the real anger is not vented constructively.

We often get this kind of misdirected anger from the two theological extremes in the pulpit. From the ultraconservative preacher who is fighting what looks like a theological battle, but is really an inner battle with himself. Often a battle to win forgiveness for what he conceives to be his own rottenness — a battle to purge his intense feeling of guilt. Or we get it from the radical social justice advocate who is not really concerned about social justice but again about his own sense of frustration in promulgating a religious faith which he has really abandoned and he feels guilty about abandoning.

2. The martyr's anger:

Example — " I don't know what to do. I have tried and tried to help you people see the importance of church attendance. We have tried to make the worship service attractive. I have tried to preach sermons on topics which you have said you were interested in. But people just don't come. What am I to do? I am trying to be your pastor, but you're fighting me. Maybe I ought to resign and let you get someone who would do a better job. I've tried, but I just don't seem to be getting anywhere."

At least the " sob sister " or martyr preacher is talking about what is bothering him — or about a part of what is bothering him. He is at least partially honest. He is bothered by poor church attendance. Of course, he is also bothered by his lack of acceptance by the people. He wants desperately to be accepted. He is dealing with his problem to a degree. He is angry and his sobbing is a kind of blowup. Perhaps it is more of a venting of frustration than of out-and-out anger. He has blown up to his wife prior to the service this morning. Now he is asking for sympathy and acceptance.

But does the preacher have a right to subject his congregation to this kind of performance? What could their reaction be? Sympathy? Perhaps they will come up to him after the service and tell him that they really do love him and that they will work harder. Will they? If they do what he seems to want, they may make him feel better, but is that so important? If the problem is low church attendance, perhaps the congregation ought to tackle that problem. And it may be that they will not tackle that problem at all because the problem which is more immediate is that of letting the preacher know that they like him. But liking the preacher would not seem to be the most crucial issue in the life of a congregation.

Some people will not react by telling the preacher they really love him and that low church attendance is not his fault. Some will resent the preacher's martyrlike attitude. They will become angry at him. They will probably talk against him behind his back and make it hard for him and for the whole congregation. Why? Because the preacher has dealt with only part of the issue. He has not helped the congregation to deal with the issue of low church attendance — an issue that should concern them more than the issue of whether or not the preacher feels accepted. Their course is diverted. The preacher has vented his frustration and anger nonconstructively.

3. Constructive anger:

Example — " I have the feeling that there is a strong undercurrent of emotion in this church on the matter of the ecumenical position that was taken at our last business meeting. As you know, I feel very strongly on this issue. As a matter of fact, I feel that we will be going against the tide of one of the major revolutions that God is directing in this world if we turn our backs on the ecumenical movement. I have expressed my views to many of you and in many of our board and committee meetings. Prior to coming into the pulpit this morning,

I talked with the deacons and we feel that it would be helpful if I brought this emotion-charged issue out in the open. I want to deal with it for the rest of the sermon time, and then we will have an opportunity in the business meeting this coming Wednesday evening to deal with it at greater length. Everyone should feel free to express his views at that time."

Notice what has happened here. The preacher has stated the issue — a strong undercurrent of emotion about the issue of ecumenicity — suggesting that this feeling has not been expressed openly. The preacher has also stated that the church, in business meeting, has at least started to face the issue, but evidently with too much haste. The preacher has expressed his emotions — "I feel very strongly." But he is not just focusing on his own feelings. He has channeled his feelings constructively by taking others into his confidence and asking for their views. He has approached boards and committees — especially the deacons. It is evident that he wants the issue dealt with by the whole church for the sake of the whole church and not just for his own sake.

The preacher showed anger in the sense that he expressed his feelings with some emotion and even hostility ("I feel that we will be going against the tide . . ."). But he did not ask the congregation to adjust to him personally. He asked the congregation to *deal with the issue.* He feels compelled to help them by giving his views and then providing them with an opportunity to express their views. It seems to me that he respects the congregation and also that he respects his own feelings.

Reaction:

"Yes, but the preacher doesn't really blow up if he does what you suggest. How does he vent his anger? How does he get rid of his frustration? "

What is more important? For the preacher to vent his anger, or for an important issue to be dealt with by a congregation?

" How should the preacher deal with his anger? "

By blowing off at his wife (if she accepts and respects him), or to himself, or to a very close friend (who is closemouthed) — but not to a congregation.

" Shouldn't anger ever be shown from a pulpit? "

If it is anger at an injustice, anger at something the congregation can do something about, anger expressed on behalf of the whole congregation. In other words, if it is honest anger about what is important to the community (not just to the preacher), and if the anger can be channeled constructively into significant action.

The Faith Crisis

Why don't we " tell it like it is "? There is a crisis of faith in this nation. There are preachers who do not believe what they are preaching. They talk about God, salvation, Jesus Christ, the power of divine love — but they don't believe it.

Not that these men are dishonest. They are preaching in an " interim age," a time between two ages. The first age was an age of belief; the age to come is an age of new belief. The old standards are dying, the new ones not yet born. And thus the preachers preach, using categories that made sense before, so that people will feel that all is not lost, that some things still matter, that the old words still have some meaning. We might as well talk about God until we find a new word. Why not speak of salvation at least until we actually move into the new era and a new word emerges? Perhaps the old words have some symbolic use, if nothing else.

Or the preachers think that they believe their old faith. It is just a passing phase — this questioning, doubting, wondering in the night if anything really matters at all anymore. Perhaps this is the cynicism and despair that goes with middle age. Growing up out of theological adolescence. Keep saying the words, singing the hymns, praying the prayers, and in time it will all go away, the gnawing doubt will cease and we will all become senior citizens in the faith.

We had dealt rather well with the crucifixion. It was a blessing in disguise, you know. Taken care of by the resurrection. Turned an instrument of torture into an instrument of love. Died that we might live. We had dealt rather well with the crucifixion.

Of course, the crucifixion was long ago, and in another country, and, besides, he is dead. But in our century six million Jews were murdered. Died that we might live? Taken care of by a resurrection? A blessing in disguise perhaps? It doesn't quite ring true, does it? Wars come and men die in Korea and Vietnam and people die needlessly and tragically and there are riots and crushed hopes and so many desperate and stupid and wicked and utterly incomprehensible and useless, useless, useless things that happen over and over again. Blessings in disguise? Tests of stamina or faith? Taken care of by a resurrection?

The Sundays come and the Sundays go and what happens? The preacher wonders if it really makes any difference, any difference at all. Who is changed? Who really cares? Why do we go through the same motions? The "last-ditch stand" is that the point of all this living is to get saved for eternity. Well, why not? It doesn't "swing" for us here in this life. Maybe God can do something after we are dead.

Is it possible that death is at the core of the experience? At least the fear of death. The fear of death is the fear of ultimate nothingness — ultimate meaninglessness. If nothingness is ultimate, it may be penultimate. If there is nothing forever, there is nothing for now. And we begin to fear that if there is nothing now, there is nothing forever. The preacher ascends to the pulpit and he says some words and he wonders — if I died right now, would it make any difference? What if I do not say these words at this time and in this place — does it make any difference? If it doesn't, then why am I here?

The faith crisis in our time is not a lack of a belief in God. It is a fear that there is nothing — nothing here and nothing forever. It is a fear that nothing matters at all in a world where people die needlessly and live uselessly. This is a loss of nerve, a loss of roots, a loss of place and of time and of identity. This is a crisis of faith.

Does It Matter?

How many times do we find ourselves talking to ourselves and asking ourselves, "Does it really matter?" All this preaching, administering, counseling, meeting, calling, teaching — all this stuff we have to do every day, every year for years and years. Does it really matter? In "the infinite scheme of things," does it really make any difference at all?

"I am afraid to sit down and ask myself if it matters. I might have to answer No."

"It is better not to ask an ultimate question like that. Just go along doing your work day by day. If you keep asking if it matters, you will go nuts."

"Of course it matters. It is God's work, isn't it?"

"We men cannot judge as to whether it matters or not. Ours not to know. Ours only to do and then leave the rest in God's hands."

D<small>IALOGUE</small>:

Mary: Why was I born, Daddy?

Daddy: You were born because Mommy and I decided that we wanted a child. So we did what was necessary to have a child. And we had you.

M.: I don't mean that. I mean why am I here? What am I here for?

D.: You mean is there any reason for your being on this earth right now?

M.: Yes. Why am I on this earth right now?

D.: Because the world needs a Mary Jackson and you are here to be Mary Jackson.

M.: But the world doesn't need me.

D.: How do you know?

M.: It got along fine without me. And anyway, I'm not doing much.

D.: The world got along fine without me too, but aren't you glad I'm here?

M.: Oh, sure, Daddy. But are you here just for me?

D.: For you and for Mommy and Sammy and for my mother and dad and for anyone I can love and help and do something for and be a friend to.

M.: I'm here for you? To be your daughter?

D.: That's one reason. It's a good one too, the way I look at it.

M.: But I must be here for more than that. Being your daughter isn't all that hard.

D.: You are here for a lot of people who love you and people who don't even know you yet. People you will meet in years to come.

M.: You mean we kids and grown-ups are all here just for each other? Like to be with each other and help each other and stuff like that? That's why we're here?

D.: It sounds good to me.

How does it sound to you? Not too religious? Not very Christian? Didn't Jesus say that we were here for each other? That he was here for us — " the man for others "? If we aren't here for each other, for whom or for what are we here? For God? I can't get too excited over the idea that God sees us as existing for him. Why does he need us? It seems to me that we need each other a great deal more than God might need us. We can do things for each other that even he can't seem to do. We can love each other with a human kind of love, and he can't seem to do that — except perhaps through people like Jesus and like us.

Does it matter? Does this life matter? To whom? To God? If you want to believe that, be my guest. It may be of help to you. Who you are and what you do matters to God. Frankly, that isn't too comforting unless you are a very lonely, isolated individual. Unless perhaps your hands are tied and you are utterly alone — in a mental-hospital ward or enslaved by a paralyzing disease that keeps you from speaking or writing. Most of us, however, want what we do, who we are, to matter to other human beings. The question is, " Does my life matter to anyone? "

It is not so much a question of whether my preaching matters or my counseling matters. The question is, " Do I matter? " Not just to God, but to my fellow human beings. Any of them. Any one, two, three, or a hundred of them.

Is it perhaps an even more important question to ask, " Do I matter to me? " Do I think that I am important? I do not think that this can be separated from the question as to whether I matter to others or not. I will matter more to me, I will seem more significant in my own eyes, if I am convinced that I matter to others. I am much more apt to love myself, to respect myself, if I am loved and respected by another. The reverse is also true. I will love others more deeply if I love myself. I have no self-image in complete isolation from what I think others think of me.

" Do I matter? " can be translated " Am I loved? " The question, " Does it matter? " means, " Can love happen? " If love can happen, then something matters.

" Is life worth living? " Another way of asking that question is, " Can anyone love me? " If someone can, then life is worth living. " Can anyone love me and can I love him? " If so, then life is worth living. If I am utterly alone, isolated, unloved, cared for by absolutely no one, then that is the end of it. Life is not worth living. I can say that at least God loves me — but it isn't much comfort. He could probably love me dead as well as alive. I want to be alive if it means that I can know what it means to be cared for and to care.

In a world where a Samaritan can bind up the wounds of a complete stranger, life is worth living. In a world where a father can run down the road to embrace his wayward son, something matters. In a world where a man can forgive his follower for betraying him — my God! — in that kind of a world love can happen. Life does not seem to be worth living in a world where six million Jews can be murdered. But life does seem to be worth living in a world where a man, Viktor Frankl, who lived through the concentration camps, can write about the value of life and can help thousands of people to find new meaning in their lives. Evil does not justify life. But love does. If love can happen — anywhere — then life matters.

Preaching is a celebration of the possibility of love. It is the celebrating of our true humanity. Preaching can matter only if it is a celebration of the realities of love. Celebration is life.

I preach in order to celebrate. As I preach, I invite you to celebrate with me the possibilities for human beings. Jesus, in spite of all that happened to him that would make most of us crack up, celebrated the fact that this world, *this* world, was the one in which love could happen. Healing could happen. People could be made whole. Is this possible? Can a human being so love another, that the other can feel the surge of wholeness, the power of life coursing through him until it spills out in joy? Is it possible that in the midst of the persecution in the Soviet Union, the old Jew can clutch the Torah in his arms and dance? Dance, mind you — not sit down and smile bravely — but *dance!*

There is a divine madness in us. Hindu mythologies describe divine beings who dance and cavort with abandon. We human beings need to dance the dance of the gods. Why dance? Because love can happen. Not because we are gods, but because we are men.

Does my life matter?

I can take my wife's hand and look into her eyes and know that she is and wants to be a part of who I am.

I can hug my son so tight and he isn't hurt.

I can speak to a fellow human being about his life and how I see him, and he will listen and wait for more, and I will feel that I am pouring out to him, and he will receive.

I can make a plant grow that would have been dead had I not planted it.

I can join an organization that can help, actually help some people who need help.

I can pray — by crying out and laughing and opening up to all that is and all that sustains and he who somehow, I know not how, knows that I am here and praying.

I matter.

To me and to others.

Amen.

IV | The Message and the Preaching Event

W<small>HEN A PREACHER</small> sits down to work on a message, he needs to be aware of the congregation (Chapter II) and of himself (Chapter III). He has to know to whom the message is directed, and he has to know who he is as a person who is trying to communicate with a congregation. Finally the hour arrives when he has to put words on paper (or into a tape recorder). What goes through his mind at such a time? The following essays set forth those thoughts which I feel should go through a preacher's mind if he is to prepare a significant message.

The first essay, "Establishing Relationship," deals with how to begin a message. The essay on "The Event" puts the message in perspective — the part it plays in the total preaching event. "Questions for Sermon Preparation" describes a method which some seminarians and myself have used with a degree of success. "What's Happening" is an evocative and pictorial response to the question What is preaching? "Application and Implication" is written from the standpoint of a member of the congregation. In "Illumination" I carry on a dialogue with myself. "The Present" is a call for church renewal through involvement in the pains and joys of living. I identify here particularly with the young person who looks at the church and wonders if it offers anything to him. "Lying" is written in a confessional manner, though it is not particularly autobiographical. I speak for some men I know who are agonizing over their vocation and are crying out for help. In the two essays on invitational preaching, a systematic attempt is made to describe a type of preaching that is relevant for our time. The essays on "Religious Language" and "Religion" are reactions to what the communications experts, the analytical philosophers, and, for that matter, the "man in the pew," are telling preachers today. In these essays I speak *to* and *for* preachers. "A Successful Sermon" reflects a personal wrestling with a question that "bugs" most preachers today. "Sensitizing" deals with the question of whether or not a preacher really has anything unique to say. The chapter ends with the essay on "Something to Take Home with You" because I have heard this plea so often from laymen and I believe that it should be taken seriously.

Establishing Relationship

I understand that when the playwright Edward Albee came to town he began his talk to a large audience with the word "Hello." Then he said something like, "There are so many of you and there is only one of me."

Techniquewise, Albee's approach could be called gaining rapport with his audience. I think, however, that it is more than that. It is more than technique, and more than rapport. He is saying: "Here I am, here you are. We need to be together and work together — I hope you will stick with me as we try to make something important happen here." He is also saying, "I am a human being, like you are, a little frightened by this large audience and by my responsibility to you — take me as a fellow human being — O.K.?"

How many preachers are humble enough or caring enough to begin a sermon this way? How many start right out with the Biblical material or a concept or with something that is about three quarters of the way down a road that we in the congregation haven't decided to take as yet?

When I come into your home, I greet you. We sit down. We chat a bit about inconsequential things like the weather or the kids or the football game. Then we get down to the business that I came to discuss with you. At the beginning, we are saying to each other that we rather like getting together, we enjoy being in each other's company, and that we have some things — surface things, not too important, but nice-to-share things — in common. I don't come into your home and immediately start " preaching " to you.

When a preacher gets up behind the pulpit, he should ask the people to let him into their homes. He should ask, ask, ask to be invited in. Not force his way in. Not assume that he has a right to be there. In other words, he needs to establish a relationship. He needs to say " Hello." To say, " There are so many of you and there is only one of me." To say, " I am a human being too and I need you in order to be a responsible person and in order to share with you."

The Event

One of the major mistakes we make as preachers is to think of " the sermon " as something that exists by itself. We speak of " preparing my sermon," " getting the sermon ready," " I preached a sermon yesterday," and " My sermon isn't coming along too well." As if the sermon were a thing — something you could look at and analyze and say, " There it is, it is good or bad, it can be gone over, dissected, fashioned, molded, put together well, or it can fall apart."

But the sermon does not exist by itself when preaching is taken seriously.

Listen to some reactions:

" Isn't he great! We really have a fine preacher there."

" What an inspiration! "

" He is so sincere."

" I really enjoyed that."

" I don't know, I guess I wasn't in the mood this morning."

" What he said was O.K., I guess."

" I disagree with him, right down the line."

" If those kids had been quiet, I could have listened a lot better."

" He tries so hard."

" It's the same old thing — be good and have faith."

Look at these reactions. The focus is not on the words that were spoken in the " sermon." The focus is on the way the preacher's personality came across or did not come across to the hearer, or on the visceral reactions of the hearer (" I really enjoyed that "), or on the mood of the hearer and his sense of guilt for not being " with it," or on the fact that the hearer hears only some words and draws his own conclusions. The preacher, you see, is never divorced from what he says. The hearer is never divorced from what he hears. To say that the " sermon " is what is communicated is absurd.

The following is a list of some of the elements that go into the event called " preaching ":

1. The sermon manuscript: full manuscript, outline, notes, or memorized material.

2. The preacher: his personality, mood, mannerisms, attitudes, appearance, relationship with the congregation; how he sees himself, his faith, his caring or lack of caring.

3. The congregation: their individual willingness to listen; their individual and group relationships to the preacher; their

moods; what has happened to them prior to the worship service, what has happened to them in the service prior to the sermon; their individual faiths, their individual histories.

4. The worship service: particularly what happens just prior to the preaching; the mood of the service; the participation of the congregation in the service; the attitude of the preacher toward what has happened in the service.

5. The physical situation: placement of the pulpit, distance between preacher and congregation, whether people look down on the preacher or up at him; what is behind the preacher (a stained-glass window, a dossal curtain, a cross); the heat or the coldness in the room; the comfortableness, or lack of it, of the pews.

6. The community: class structure; expectations regarding the role of religion; racial character; current tensions; location of the church building in relation to the living areas; acceptance or rejection or ignoring by the community of the particular church in which the preaching is taking place.

Do you see what I mean? Is it coming through more clearly now? Preaching is an *event*. It is an event that includes a number of elements. Perhaps an infinite number. The "sermon" is but one element. When a person prepares to preach, he not only prepares a sermon, he prepares himself, the congregation, the worship service, the physical situation, and, to a degree, the community. But there is a limit to the preparing that he can do. He has more control over the sermon than anything else. This is probably why he thinks of it as the main element. He has much less control over the other elements. This scares him. He can control his own personality, to a degree, but he finds it difficult to control the congregation's reaction to him. Perhaps it is just as well. He has some power over the details of the worship service, but not much power for determining the meaning of worship for the congregation. If he is lucky, he may have some power over the physical situation. But the "layout" of the sanctuary is usually inherited. He does not have control over the community, or, at least, very little.

It is a frightening experience to enter into the preaching event. A preacher needs to enter in faith. He doesn't know what will happen. He can condition what will happen to only a very limited extent.

Questions for Sermon Preparation

I must come up with a sermon. Next Sunday looms up in front of me. I have a topic. The topic is "Discipleship." What questions must I ask myself as I prepare this sermon?

1. "Why do I care about discipleship?"

Response: I think that we in the churches are not as committed as we should be to following Jesus. But why do I care personally about discipleship? I think that I am not as committed as I should be. I go my own way and make my own plans and if the church fits into what I am planning, that is fine. If not, so much the worse for the church. But why should I personally want to be committed, to be a disciple? Because I can't go it alone. Life is not that meaningful if I see it as my little isolated task. But is that true? When have I known it to be true? I remember when I had about given up on making any sense out of the idea that God exists. It made no sense to me. I couldn't find him. I *could* find people, I could see people, people had needs that I could sense. But how about God — where was he? Then I was reading about one man's view of prayer. I tried praying again. I realized that even if I couldn't see God or sense his presence, I needed to cry out to him and I needed to feel that I was not alone. I prayed to God out of desperation and out of a deep need for his presence. I care about discipleship because I have found that I cannot " go it alone." I have to follow a path that leads from God to me and from me to God. This path has to be shown to me. I cannot create it on my own. Maybe I could tell the people about this experience.

2. "Why should the congregation care about discipleship?"

Response: Because none of us can "go it alone." We all need to be connected somehow with He who is greater than any one of us. But how do I know that anyone in this congregation feels that he cannot go it alone? I know that there are some young people in this congregation who want to be committed to something greater than themselves. They want to "give" themselves to something. Perhaps also to someone. I know that there are parents in this congregation who want to feel that who they are and what they are doing as parents is somehow of ultimate significance. Or, they want to feel that they are moving down a path that leads them to some place, some place that is "right" for them. There are people here who want to "follow." What happens if a person doesn't care about discipleship? If I don't care, then I am saying that either I have the insight, the wisdom, the strength to go it alone or I am saying that I will make the best of whatever happens — I have no direction. I will just try to live day-by-day and hope that it turns out all right. These are both dead-end streets. I know, if I am honest with myself, that I do not have the wisdom to figure things out by myself, and that I do not have the strength to "play God." I also know that I can't live day by day without some sense of direction, some sense of it all counting for something.

3. "What do we do about it if we want to be disciples?"

Response: I would say that I should recognize my need — we should all recognize our need. We need to turn to someone for help. That someone is God. This God has already turned to us — in Jesus. We try to find out how Jesus has walked the road of meaningful living. Then we turn to each other to find out what this means to other people. What have they found that makes sense to us? Or even if it doesn't make sense to us, why does it make sense to them? We commit ourselves to following Jesus — which means learning as much as we can about him — which means commitment to each other, to a common search — which means to take our own lives seriously — which means to admit to God as often as needed that we are not God and that we need help.

4. " Do I need to preach this now, this Sunday? Do I want to preach it, am I on fire with it? "

Response: Write your own.

What's Happening

1. Suppose that you are in a prison. You are all prisoners. You come together in an assembly. One of your fellow prisoners stands up and tells about how he is adjusting to life in prison — how rotten it is, how he feels about it in his guts, what few glimpses of hope he has discerned. He sits down. What would be your reaction to what happened? I might react by thinking: " I am glad to know that someone else has many of the same feelings about prison life as I do. I was kind of afraid to admit how I felt about it. Now I think I will feel freer to express myself. Actually, I've found a couple of more rays of hope that this guy hasn't found yet. Why not tell the others about it? " A number of the men might feel as I do. The prisoners would feel that the man who got up to speak had a right to take up their time. They were all interested in what he had to say. They responded to it inside of themselves. Why? For one thing, the man who got up was one of them. If you were there, you would feel that you shared something in common with him — you were all in prison. The man talked about

common problems. He spoke for all of you. He expressed what all of you felt. Hopefully you would now be given the opportunity to express yourself. He started the ball rolling. You were grateful to him because he helped you to believe that you were not so different — you share a common humanity. You would be grateful because you would feel that perhaps you could speak of what was " bugging " you.

2. Think of yourself as part of a group. You are met to hear a speaker. You don't know much about him except that he is working in some rough neighborhoods in town. He stands up before you and says something like this: " I want to tell all of you about what is happening. I've been where it's at, where it's going on. There are people in your city who are finding out that they are human beings. We are finding a group of people in the poverty area of your city who are banding together to fight city hall, who are up in arms about the conditions in which they have to live. I know these people. I live in this area. I know that these people had lost hope. They weren't willing to walk down to the office and pick up the welfare check — they sent the son down. They wouldn't lift a finger for anyone, including themselves. But now they feel that they are going to be heard. They feel that they have power. You see, a few days ago they picketed a landlord, and he made improvements in one of the apartment buildings. Now they have a sense of power. They believe that they can do something, that maybe they are worth something. Friends, this is where it is happening. The people in my part of town are excited about what can happen. We can amount to something. We can fight city hall, and no one is going to put us down again."

How would you react to this speaker? One person might say to himself: " I never thought anything could happen in the poverty area. This sounds like it is really something. Maybe there's hope after all. Maybe people can change. Maybe you can fight city hall." Another person might say to himself: "We can't have this kind of thing going on. These people ought to be law-abiding. They shouldn't demonstrate or picket. I'm mad. I think we ought to tell this guy that we don't approve of what he's doing."

However you might react, at least we could say that you listened to this speaker. Why? Because he was on fire with something. He was involved in something that excited him. He was speaking of what was real, vital, alive, and firsthand. He was talking about real life. He was telling you what was actually happening. And he interpreted the events so that you would gain insight into what was happening. Yet his interpretation was not forced on the situation, but, rather, grew out of the situation. It was his way of saying what he thought the "happening" meant. As listeners, you might identify with him and be thankful that human beings can change and can sense their self-worth. This might give you hope. Or you might get upset and react against the whole thing. Particularly if you felt personally threatened by poverty groups rising up and demanding something from you. You wouldn't be neutral to this speech or speaker. You would probably react.

3. You are a part of a small group of people meeting in a building. It is a business meeting. All of a sudden there is a knock on the door of the room. The door is opened and a man bursts in, all out of breath. He cries out: "I have to get to a phone and call the police. A woman is being beaten up and maybe raped. Could someone run down there and help her while I phone? Please — she is being hurt something awful. Where's a phone?"

How would you react to this? One person might shout, "Follow me, I'll take you to a phone." Another might say, "Let's all go out there and beat 'em up." Some might say to themselves: "I'd better sit quietly and let the others take off.

Then I can sneak out. I don't want to get mixed up in this."
All of these people are reacting to the speaker. They are not
neutral. You would have to make a decision either to be involved or not to be. You would care about what happened.
You would react intellectually and emotionally. Why? Because the man who came in and brought you the message —
the challenge — was speaking about what was real. You had
to make a decision. No one else knew about the problem. The
speaker cared about what he was telling you. He obviously
needed help — he could not deal with the situation by himself.
He invited you to do something that was very specific.

What is preaching? It is sharing with your brothers what is
real to you. It is stimulating your brothers to speak of what is
real to them. It is thanksgiving for being human. It is telling
people where life is being lived. It is spreading the word that
things are happening in this world that are important. Preaching is celebrating our common humanity. It is celebrating our
common mission. It is stimulating people to get up and get
with it. It is telling people who we are, and where it is, and
who they are, and asking them to be who they are at a particular time and in a particular place.

Application and Implication

Preachers usually present us with a truth that is to be ap-
plied to our lives. A text is given, explained, and then ap-
plied. But isn't this method totally in opposition to the way we
do and should live?

I don't take a truth and apply it to my life. Why should I
try to so rearrange or open up a hole in my life in order that
a truth can find a place to lodge? Isn't it more valid to say that
I need to examine my life? Look at my life, the way I am ac-

tually living it. Take my life seriously. And then ask the question, What is implied by my living?

For example: My attitude toward my friends. What is implied in this? I speak to them civilly. What does this mean? Does it mean that I care about them? Or does it mean that I acknowledge their presence? That depends on how I speak to them, doesn't it? I speak to one friend, and I tell him what agony I am now facing. I speak to him feelingly and rationally of my understanding of myself and my feeling. I ask for his help. What is implied in this? That I love him? Perhaps at least that I need him and that I know that I do.

The application-oriented person might say: "You should love your friends. Now apply this principle to your relationships." The implication-oriented person might say: "How are you treating your friends? What is implied by your treating of them? How can you amplify that which is helpful, encouraging, and life-giving? How can you play down that which turns you away from your friends?"

I often think that instead of a preacher talking all the time as if he knew what I needed, it would help if he listened to me as I told him of my life. Then he could ask some probing questions. Then he could point out some implications of my way of living. Isn't this preaching? — the probing word, the word that illumines my living and puts it into perspective. How can he find a word that speaks to me unless he knows me, asks me about my living, finds out what I am doing and feeling and worrying about and am happy for?

Perhaps it would help if the preacher would tell me, from the pulpit, what he conceives to be the implications of the lives with which he is familiar. Even what he thinks is implied by his own living. I could "connect" with that. I could feel with him then. He speaks from *within* living and not from *outside* of living *to* it. The gospel must be something that comes alive in our living of life, not something that is thrown at us from a world beyond. It is a proclamation within the midst of living. A proclamation that helps to dispel the mist, or at least to make it bearable.

Let the preacher speak of living, of what is really going on. Not about some truth that exists "out there" in limbo. Jesus didn't speak of something "out there." He spoke of what is implied in living. He would look at some Pharisees and draw the implications of their living. He looked at the demoniac and said the man was sick and needed healing. Jesus took people seriously. He looked at them and how they were living and he did not fit them into categories. They were not receptacles into which he poured time-honored truths. What is Israel doing? Here is the meaning of what she is doing. Not here is a truth that Israel should apply to her life. Not "here is a truth, start applying it, start now or you are naughty."

It is so much easier, of course, to say, in a blanket statement, "Here is what he should be doing." "John should really pull himself together" (the assumption being that if all people could only pull themselves together the millennium would come). What the hell do you know about what John should do? Deal with John, live with him, agonize with him, and then, maybe, but only maybe, and only if John really wants you to, you can say what you think his living implies. Then he will know that you care. And this will hit him hard. He won't listen to you if you hand him truths. But if you care — if you see your living as somehow tied up with his living — he will listen. True caring is something he must deal with. He may say, "No, stay away," but he must deal with it.

Illumination

A: Do you believe in preaching from the Bible?

B: Definitely. We need to know what is in the Bible.

A: Do we? You mean we need to know what the Bible means?

B: Certainly. Don't you think so?

A: No.

B: What do you mean, no?

A: I mean that I am not primarily concerned with what the Bible means.

B: What are you concerned about?

A: I am concerned about what life means, and, specifically, my life and the lives of those close to me.

B: That sounds nice, but I don't quite see why you reject the Bible.

A: I don't reject the Bible. I just think it should be used properly.

B: What do you mean by properly?

A: I think the Bible is valid only as it illumines our lives, probes our lives, helps us to find out what is going on within us and helps us to live more fully and truthfully.

B: Don't you discover this by finding out what the Bible says?

A: In a way. But I am sick and tired of preachers who spend so much time "illumining the text." It is as if shedding light on the meaning of the Bible passage was what was important. It isn't illumining the text that is important, it is whether or not the text illumines our lives. The text is a tool for analyzing life and helping to guide our living.

B: You mean that it isn't a matter of finding out what the Bible means, but a matter of finding out what the Bible says about our living?

A: O.K. Except that the Bible " means " what it teaches us about our living. The Bible doesn't have a " meaning " of its own, all by itself, in isolation from our living. The meaning of the Bible comes through *only* when it is used to illumine our lives. That is the only meaning it has.

B: I'm a bit lost. Give me an example.

A: All right. Let's take a text. How about the one I used last Sunday? Luke 21:1-4. Here it is. I'll read it to you.

He looked up and saw the rich putting their gifts into the treasury; and he saw a poor widow put in two copper coins. And he said, " Truly I tell you, this poor widow has put in more than all of them; for they all contributed out of their abundance, but she out of her poverty put in all the living that she had."

How is that for a text?

B: Not bad. You preached a stewardship sermon last Sunday — right?

A: Not exactly. But sort of, yes.

B: Continue.

A: All the business about the furnishings of the Temple in Jerusalem is irrelevant, as is the information about the practice of contributing money to the Temple. Who the rich were, who the widow represents — who cares? I don't think Jesus cared. He is using this instance to point up something about life. Not about life in general — about life in Jerusalem at that time and among the people to whom he was speaking. Now let's look at us. We are giving money to various causes — right? We give money to the church, the Boy Scouts, the P.T.A., the United Fund. What are we doing? We are giving money. But the text suggests that we ask ourselves a probing question — Are we giving out of our abundance or out of our poverty? Most of us would say out of our abundance. But so what? What difference does it make? The text probes deeper.

The widow put in all the living she had. Do we put in all our living? What does this mean — all our living? Does it mean that we need to ask ourselves if we put all our money into worthy causes? No. I think the text is asking us if we put our*selves* — all our living — into those efforts we have labeled as good and worthy. Isn't this a valid question to ask? The basic question is not, What should I give to the church, the Boy Scouts, the P.T.A., the United Fund? The basic question is, What am I giving when I give to any cause? Or, Am I giving myself? This is tremendously important. How often do we give our *selves* to anything? When we give money to something, do we follow through by giving ourselves? Or do we escape from giving ourselves by giving money? There is something even more important here. The New Testament pictures Jesus as a self-giver. This picture must be the key to living as Jesus saw it. This must be what it means to be human. We should rejoice in this. We can give our*selves*. Amazing? Indeed. A cause for celebration. Not a time for saying, " Gee, I really ought to give more to the church." Rather, a time for saying, " My God, I can actually give of myself to people and to organizations and then I can live and this is what it means to be human — I can do it. I can actually live a life that is real life! "

B: This is what you mean by the text illumining life?

A: Right.

B: The text asks probing questions. It provides a way of digging into the meaning of our living. Right?

A: Right.

B: But why use the Bible? Why not some other text?

A: I think that it is in the Bible that God has asked the probing questions, that he has addressed men with the words that we need to hear — not actually in the Bible itself, of course, but in the events — the experiences recorded in the Bible. The Bible points us to God's authoritative questioning and probing.

It asks the questions that need to be asked. I take this stand. Why? I suppose because I have found help there. I need a star to guide me. And I think that a great many people have had light shed on the meaning of their lives by this book. I believe that I need help from outside of myself. I will not generally question my living unless I am questioned.

B: The text addresses us. Or you could say that God addresses us through the text. Yet it isn't the text that is important, but the address. The text has instrumental importance. It is a way of addressing us. And you think that it is the authoritative way?

A: Unless the text illumines our lives, I can pretty well do without it. But I would also hold that if the text does not appear to illumine our lives on first examination, then I cannot necessarily leave it alone. I need to look again and again at other times and in future circumstances and see if perhaps then, in that time and place, I am being addressed by this text which did not speak to me before.

The Present

Preaching could be considered as a calling to mind or recounting of the past. A rehearsal of the mighty acts of God in past history. But this type of preaching does not " grab " many of us today.

"Grab": To take hold of, wake up, shake, break out of lethargy.

We are tired of the past. The past is a burden, not a release. It can be an escape. As if we had never been forgiven.

DIALOGUE (in a prison):

Inmate A: Who are you, man? Why are you in here? What's your " bag "?

Inmate B: I'm here because I held up a guy five years ago

and he was a big deal in this town and they hit me for thirty years. I was " had."

A: What are you doing about it?

B: I'm going to make it. I'm going to get out, and I'm going to make it.

A: How do you know you're going to make it?

B: I've got to make it. It's bad in here.

A: What have you been doin' to make it out there?

B: I've been thinking a lot and I know I'm going to make it.

A: But why? Why? Why do you know now that you're going to make it? Why didn't you make it before?

B: I was had. They made me fall.

A: That don't make any difference. That's done. That's all over, man. How are you going to make it now?

B: I don't know, but I'm going to make it.

Making it now is what we are about and is what it is all about. When you or I get up to preach, we better talk about making it *now*. If we don't, then people will escape into thinking about who made it in the past or they just won't listen because they only know or care about now. You and I have to do something, however, before we can talk about making it now.

We have to make it now.

I can't tell someone what it is like to make it, to live it, to be it now, unless I know, unless I am making it, unless I am living it, unless I *am* it — *now*. Unless life is breaking out for me now, unless something is happening to me now so powerfully that I can't hold it in, unless I am involved in making it (meaning, purpose, vitality, significance) now, I cannot preach to anyone today — because I have nothing to say, nothing that helps them to make it where they are with who they are.

If we can't make it together, we aren't going to make it at all. This was what happened in the first-century church —

they made it together. They couldn't have done it separately. But a lot of people today don't know this. They don't know that " making it " is something you need other people for. Unless somehow a lot of people, or maybe even everyone (though that sounds pretty idealistic), is making it, no one is. " It " is a life, a whole thrust of existing that we make together. Or it isn't being made at all. Like in a church where people come individually to worship God and hear a sermon and walk out. That isn't a church. That isn't making it. That is a building that is there so that individuals can come in out of the weather. A real church is a group of people who know that they can't make it separately and have to make it together or it isn't made at all.

When I hear a preacher, I want to know that he is alive now, that he is living now, that he is moving with what is going on now, and that he wants me and all the people here in this place with me to be alive and making it with him now. To put it Biblically, Jesus is Lord now, living Lord, or he is no Lord at all. When he is Lord of a people now, this people is alive and this people is his body — the only body he has now.

Lying

Do preachers lie? That is a horrible thought, isn't it? All that awesome responsibility and the man is lying to you?

I went to heaven and after a reasonable waiting period I was ushered into the holy of holies to appear before He who is. He seemed worried. I had never thought of God as a worrier. He had a sheaf of papers in front of him. He turned to me and inquired, " You're a pastor, aren't you? " I confessed that I had been a pastor on earth. He said, " I wish you would look at these confessions, written by your fellow professionals." I picked up a slip of paper and read these words:

" I confess that I have told people for years that if they would only confess their sins and accept Jesus Christ as their personal Savior, they would be in good shape. But I have been lying to them. I don't know if confessing their sins and accepting Christ puts them in good shape or not. I have confessed my sins and I have honestly tried to follow Jesus, but I haven't always been in good shape. In fact, I have felt rotten and even lived rotten at times. Who am I to guarantee that if people confess and follow, they will be set for heaven? What a ridiculous thing to do — to guarantee that. I have known people — not just me — who have said that they confessed and accepted Christ as their Savior (I have no reason to doubt them) and they were, at least in my estimation, messing up their lives to an alarming degree. I cannot guarantee anything to people. But I have. I lied to them. I lied to myself."

I looked at God and he said, " What do you think? " I answered, " Well, at least he is honest now — that's something, isn't it? " God said, " Yes, and perhaps that is all I can expect in his case. Look at another one of these confessions." I read as follows:

" I confess that I have ascended the pulpit Sunday after Sunday and have told people how wonderful it is to live the Christian life and what rewards it brings, and I have not felt that it is very wonderful. Either that, or I haven't really been living a Christian life. I have spent my working life worrying about meeting budgets, getting people out to meetings, making our church known in the community, and all my worrying has driven me to an early grave. I have not been a free man, and yet how often I have preached about Christ setting us free as Christians. My God, what have I done? I have talked about something I have not experienced, or experienced only in snatches of time. I have misled people time and again. One time a young person in my church came up to me after a revival meeting and said that she had found Jesus and that she felt free and at peace. I took her hand and said, 'Isn't that wonderful? Thank God!' And for years afterward I would tell about this young person — how she had found freedom and peace and how, therefore, all of you out there in the congregation could find freedom and peace too if you would only let God take over in your lives. I lived as a preacher for years on that girl's faith. Six years ago she divorced her husband. Or, rather, he divorced her. She was driving him crazy, going from one religious cult to the next, trying to find peace of mind. My prime example was gone. I was building my preaching ministry on quicksand. I have lied to people all of my life."

I found an excuse to leave God about this time. I was afraid he might expect a confession from me and discover that I was in the wrong place.

What Kind of Preaching Is Needed Today

We need to do three things in preaching: First, we need to direct our preaching to men and women at the point of their basic needs. We need to speak to people about their lives, and about the great needs of their lives. Second, we are bound by Christ to shed the light of the gospel on the matter of human need. We need the gospel in order that we may understand the nature and significance of our true needs, and in order that we may be given hope. Preaching is bringing light into the darkness. Third, we need to challenge people to live the life that Jesus offers to us — to follow the light and realize the hope of the gospel. We as preachers are called to invite people into life. Preaching focuses on *need, gospel, invitation*. I call this kind of preaching " invitational preaching " — preaching that invites men and women to enter into life in God's world. Such preaching is invitational from beginning to end.

We invite people to see their own needs; we invite them to see their needs in the light of the gospel; and we invite them to respond to the call of Jesus to live in the world. We invite people to follow Jesus, to follow him where he leads them, to follow him into the life of this world, to follow him where he is at work in this world. Preaching is invitation.

The first task that is set before us in invitational preaching is to speak to people at the point of their basic needs. The alternative to starting with human need is, of course, to start with the Bible, with a particular passage of Scripture, and then apply it to contemporary life. It is my belief that most people today, even people in Christian congregations, and even people who have grown up in Christian homes and have come up through the church school are not asking Biblical questions. They are not concerned with an exposition of Biblical truth in the sense of wondering what the story of Joseph says to our time, or even what the view that Jesus is the Son of God says to our situation. They are not asking Biblical questions such as, What does God require of us? or, What does Jesus want me to do? People today are asking about their lives. They are asking about the significance of their own existence.

We are living in a time when people, even Christian people, do not assume that the gospel deals with their real problems. Their interest in the Bible is essentially a practical interest — how the Bible can deal with their problems. Up to a point they may be interested in exegetical matters such as who do Cain and Abel represent, or how valid are the birth stories of Jesus. But these problems soon become not much more than interesting games to play.

We should begin at the point of human need — where Jesus began — with a rich young man who was worried about the meaning of his life, with a lawyer who did not know which way to turn, with a woman who had had too many husbands, with disciples who wanted rewards for their faithfulness, with the Pharisees who desired to justify their self-righteousness, with the lame, the blind, the oppressed, the poor. We begin with human need.

In the second place, invitational preaching is concerned with bringing the light of the gospel to bear on the needs of people In Jesus Christ, the gospel of life, God is saying: " I have seen the affliction of my people, and have heard their cry. I know their sufferings, and I have come down to deliver them." Invitational preaching is concerned with relating the gospel of God to the needs of people.

Jesus came to those in need. He healed them. He made the lame walk and the blind see. But he went deeper than this and spoke of the need of the people for a faith, a hope, a quality of living that would enable them to live with each other in love. After the blind man can see, at what does he look? After the lame man can walk, where does he go? The gospel sheds light on men's true needs — not just on those needs we think we have, but on those deeper needs of which we may not even be aware. This is Biblical preaching, not in the sense of taking a text and making it relevant to the needs of men and women. But it is Biblical preaching in that we start where people are and then show them what the Biblical witness has to say to them where they are. In a way this is using the Bible to deal with men's problems. But it is more than this. For the Bible is not something that can be taken like a medicine. The Bible challenges; it challenges us to dig deeper and look at who we really are, from God's perspective and not just our own.

I firmly believe that people would be more apt to listen to preachers if they came to realize that the gospel deals with their true needs and not with some artificially induced needs or with needs that seem to be limited to first-century Palestine. It is our responsibility to say to anyone who will give us even

" half an ear " that man's need is dealt with in the gospel. If we do not believe this, then we have nothing to say.

The third element in invitational preaching is invitation. We cannot say to people that we sense their needs, that the gospel sheds light on their needs, and then stop. If we leave the matter there, we have not fulfilled our responsibility. Ours is a practical age. We are a practical people. There is a way to meet our true need. Fine. How? At what time and in what place can we do this? We want the preacher to be specific, not to preach generalities. Certainly we do not want to preach faith, faith, faith, hope, hope, hope, without at some point dealing with the time for faith, the place for faith, the reason for holding out hope in a particular situation in human life.

We have somehow gotten the idea that the main thing that people have to do in this world in order to find meaning in life is to accept Jesus Christ as their personal Savior. Some preachers have given us the idea that if we accept Christ as our Savior, then we shall automatically enter into life. The only invitation that is given in many of our churches today is the invitation to come forward and accept Christ — as if this were all that Jesus desired, all that God wanted us to do, all that we needed to do in order to find meaning in life! But this invitation to accept him as Savior is only one aspect of Jesus' invitation. When Jesus called his disciples, he did not say, " Come over here and accept me as your personal Savior." He said, " Follow me." This meant, literally, to get up and walk with him, to go where he was going, to follow him down the road. When he healed the paralytic, he did not say, " Accept me as your personal Savior." He said, " Take up your bed and walk." Jesus, in fact, asked for an acceptance of him on the part of the disciples *after* they had already begun to follow him. It was not until the eighth chapter of Mark that Jesus asked, " Who do you say that I am? " When Peter blurted out that he was the Messiah, Jesus told him to keep silent about it. This particular understanding of Jesus as the Anointed One, as the Savior, is something about which Jesus said little. No doubt, it was because he felt that it would be misleading, that people would read a lot of things into Messiahship or Saviorhood.

Today, our invitation to people is an invitation to follow Jesus. When we talk about following him, we need to be specific. Jesus was always specific. Harvey Cox in *The Secular City* (p. 122; The Macmillan Company, 1965) reminds us that Jesus " expected people to drop their nets, get out of bed, untie a horse, invite him to dinner. No one could doubt either that something momentous had occurred or that something quite definite was required of him." To follow Jesus is to engage in specific actions. It is not to sit around and feel like a follower, to sit around and be glad that one is " saved." It is rather difficult to follow, if we are not moving. But to pinpoint, to be specific, is to run a risk that preachers often do not want to run. It is " risky business," this matter of being specific. We could be wrong. We could lead people on lost causes. We could incur the wrath of well-meaning men of high position.

Helmut Thielicke, the great contemporary German preacher, tells of a dream that he had during the time of the Nazi rule in Germany:

I imagined a demonstration in the Berlin Sportplast put on by the German Faith Movement with the appropriate anti-Christian agitation. As the hate tirades reached their climax, a Christian in the audience could stand it no longer. He felt that he must stand up and declare himself and he loudly shouted out, " Christ is the Messiah." In the rows of seats in front of him — I imagined — a few people turned around to look with surprise at the interrupter only to turn away again from this presumed zealot and concentrate their attention upon the platform. But there was another who spoke out somewhat more clearly. He shouted, " Christ is the only Lord and Leader and without him Hitler and all the apostles of this false faith will go to hell." This man was mobbed and torn to pieces, for that exclamation, God knows, " hit home." (*The Trouble with the Church,* p. 37; Harper & Row, Publishers, Inc., 1965).

At some point, we have to get specific. If Christ is Lord, if we say we are to follow him, then at what time and in what place do we do it?

What Kind of Preachers Are Needed Today

Since it is the preacher who does the preaching, we cannot divorce the sermon from the one who sermonizes, the preaching from the preacher. If preaching is to be invitational, what kind of preachers does this require?

First of all, if we are going to start with people at the point of their need, we preachers are going to have to know what are the needs of people in our day. I do not mean to know these needs in an abstract sense, that is, to know *about* them. We preachers need to identify with people in need. We have to stand where our people stand. Some preachers have difficulty in doing this, for they have become infatuated with the image of success. They assume that a minister should appear to be successful in having overcome most of the major problems of life. But people do not expect much help or understanding from a man such as this. Instead, they feel apart from him, perhaps not good enough for him. He may preach about victorious living and how we can conquer all problems, but he seems to be living in a world apart, in another dimension. He seems to be other than human. If we preachers are going to speak to people in need, we better recognize that not only must

we stand with our people, but that *we already do stand with them* if we would only admit it.

Not only must we stand with people in need if we are to speak to them, but we must ask people what they feel their needs to be. We have to ask people in the church concerning the needs that they feel. Indeed, we are going to have to ask people to come to church to express their needs. I do not mean only the religious people. I mean all kinds of people. The doors of the church should be open to all people. We should listen, even within the walls of the church, to those whom we do not like, to the atheists and the agnostics, to the offbeat, the different, the poor, the " have-nots " and the " has-beens." Our churches must be " listening posts," places where people of all kinds feel that they can talk about what is really bothering them without fear of being cut off or rejected.

However, it is unrealistic to assume that everyone will come to the church and express his needs. At some point we have to go outside the doors and move into the places where most of the people live and work. We cannot live our lives as preachers, or even as laity for that matter, within the sacred precincts. The world passes by. The world, though it cares little for the church, cares desperately about life, about meaning and purpose in life. If we care about the needs of men, let us go to men and women and discover their needs.

Secondly, if we are to be the kind of preachers who are needed today we shall have to be men and women who know from " firsthand experience " what it is to lose our lives. It is both dishonest and impossible to speak to men of the gospel unless we have experienced the power of the gospel in our own lives. Unless we have known moments when we have moved out of our narrowness, have lost our lives in service to our brothers, have given as fully of ourselves as we know how and have found our lives given to us from God's hands, unless we can say with conviction and out of our own experience, " I know what Jesus means when he says, ' He who loses his life for my sake and the gospel's shall find it ' " — unless we can do this, then we preach as hypocrites. We preach as people who can only say, " Now I personally do not know what it means to have found new life, but I commend it to you nonetheless and good luck to you." How can we commend the gospel to anyone unless we have known something of its power in our own lives?

We need more people than just the preachers who can do what we have been calling for. Our churches must be places where at least some men and women, laity as well as preachers, can speak of their having walked with Jesus. The man who gets up into the pulpit on Sunday morning and evening cannot be the only preacher in the church. People today expect the pastor to have walked with Jesus, but they are often shocked to discover that some laymen have also walked with him. Even the preacher seems to be shocked at times. The preacher can say a lot from the pulpit about firsthand experience with life, but when a layman says it, in a church school class, or a board meeting, or at a meal, or at work, or even from the pulpit, then people often sit up and listen. We must give laymen a chance to be preachers, to tell others of their losing of their lives. This is " testimony." But it is not just testimony about having been converted on such and such a day at such and such a time. I am more concerned with testimony from laymen that they have walked with Jesus in the office, the factory, among their families, in the community, in their attempts to right the wrongs in society, in the places of illness, in the situations of poverty, in any place where there is human need. Other laymen will identify with fellow laymen more than they ever will with the preacher, human as he is and as they know him to be. Preaching in the church and in the community is not confined to those who get paid for it. We need preachers, both lay and professional, who are willing to speak of what they have experienced.

Let us go even deeper. Let us state that if we have found something, if we have known in our own experience what it means, at least in some measure, to lose our lives, *then we must sense the urgency* of helping others to lose their lives. If we believe that men and women can move out of " lostness," can move beyond giving up the battle for meaning and purpose in life, can actually come to some sense of worth, to some understanding of the importance of their lives and the importance of the lives of all of us, then we should recognize the urgency of speaking to people of this hope. We are not just " playing around." We are not conducting religious " fun and games." If there is such a thing as a new creation in Christ Jesus, a new life that comes in following him, a new birth that comes from losing one's life, then people must know it, and know it from firsthand experience. If they do not, are they not lost to life? All of us, even those of us who call ourselves Christians, are like dead people if we live only for ourselves, or if we have given up the fight for life and act as if nothing is important anymore. There is an urgency about this matter of the gospel's answer to our needs. How about us? Are we living? Has the gospel spoken to our needs? Have we responded? Have we found life in following Jesus? If so, let us shout it out. If not, let us get down from our pulpits and go into some other line of work. Unless we have met Jesus on the road and have experienced something of the loss of life and the receiving of life that comes from walking with him, we have nothing to say to anyone.

Thirdly, if we are to be preachers in the sense in which I have been using the term, then we have to study the Bible and Christian thought. Why? Because as real as our experience of

Jesus may be, if we guide our lives solely by what we suppose to be true on the basis of our limited experience, we are playing God to ourselves. We need to submit our experiences to the judgment of God, to the judgment of his revelation in Christ as recorded in the Bible, and to the combined judgment of the experiences of his followers throughout the history of the church. We preachers need to consider these matters not only in the quiet of our study, but with our people, as all of us together study the Bible and Christian thought. We must all recognize that we do not stand alone as the first people who have ever known what it is to live. Others have known it too. The Gospel writers knew, Paul knew, Augustine knew, Luther knew. We have much to learn from them. We need a light that is not merely our own light. We need a light that has been illuminating in times past as well as in our own time. We are not our own saviors. If we are to follow Jesus, we need to know of the witness to him by people in many times, in many places. Otherwise we follow our own star, our own little lights, and soon we will find ourselves groping in the darkness. We need to study the Bible and the history of Christian thought and experience.

Fourthly, if we are to invite people to follow Jesus in specific ways, then we need to know of some times and some places when and where he can be followed. We need to be so aware of our church and our community, indeed, of the whole world in which we live, that we can say to people: " I believe that Jesus is there, in that place, at this time, let us run after him and lose our lives." This will involve our submitting our church's program, its activities, its organization, to the judgment of Jesus. Are these things which we are doing in our churches really significant? Are the times we announce, the places where we ask people to go, the meetings we ask them to attend, the programs we ask them to support — are these the times, places, meetings, programs where Jesus can be followed? Does the church provide times and places where we can lose our lives? Or does the church spend a lot of time in matters that help us only a little bit, or that are interesting but not very challenging, or even that deepen our sense of helplessness or reinforce our unchristian prejudices?

The laity are needed at this point as they have been needed all along the way. We preachers do not know all that is going on in the church and in the community. We do not know all the times and places where Jesus can be followed, even within our own churches. We need church people who will tell us if they are discovering in the church ways of moving beyond the rat race. We need to be told if people are challenged in any specific church program to lose their lives. Furthermore, we need " reporters " from our church to go into the community and find out where the significant events are taking place. Indeed, we preachers need to be where things are happening. What are young people doing in our city that is of real worth to other people? Let us find out and go there to help them. What sort of action is being taken to help people of different races to learn to live together? Let us support that action. We have to know, we have to ask the laity to tell us " where the action is," both in the church and in the community. We need " spies " to look at the territory around us and come back and say, " I think Jesus is leading us in this direction. How about some of us going there and finding out? " Where can we give ourselves? In this respect, I do not mean just giving money to missions or to the community chest, for so often that is laying our purses on the line but not our lives. I mean at what points in the community can we pick up our feet and walk? " Be good and have faith " does not go very far in our time. Few people are fooled by such platitudes anymore. If the preacher is to be specific about the times and the places where

Jesus can be followed, he has to know of those times and those places.

Religious Language

Should we actually use a religious language at all? Certain words such as " salvation," " redemption," " sin," " theological," " divine," " spiritual," " worldly," perhaps even " God " and " Jesus Christ," are used almost exclusively in a religious context. These are words we hear in church, but we seldom hear them otherwise. Is this significant?

Let me tell you about an experience I had recently. I was a member of a " T-group." A group of people sat around and talked to each other about how we felt about our individual lives and how we felt about each other. It was very exciting. I learned a lot about myself and also about other people — at least those in the group. We were all professional religious types — seminarians, professors, ministers. All of us were used to using religious language. But do you know that in the whole two days we hardly ever used a religious word? I would say that " God " was mentioned perhaps three times, " Christ " one time, and I do not believe that any of the religious words mentioned in the paragraph above were used except, possibly, " theological." When we were talking about what was most important to us, we wanted desperately to communicate. And when we wanted to communicate, we did not use religious words. It wasn't because we were ignorant of such words. It was just that they didn't seem relevant.

Instead of using the word " salvation," we spoke of getting to know people more deeply and getting to understand ourselves more fully. Instead of " redemption," we spoke of caring about other people, really being concerned. Instead of " sin," we spoke of self-hate, hurting the other person, treating another person as a thing. Instead of " theological," we spoke of being intellectual or impersonal, and we talked of the need of seeing ourselves as whole persons. Instead of "divine," we spoke of not knowing how to express what we feel, of trying to reach out toward another person. Instead of "worldly," we spoke of caring about what happens here and now, caring about people with whom we come into contact.

Why do we use religious language in preaching? Do we think that if we do so we speak with more authority? There is some truth in this, no doubt, in that many people expect religious language in sermons and they think that if they hear the religious words (salvation, blood, sin, washed clean, divine guidance, etc.) they are hearing the voice of God. But are they? What is communicated by hearing a religious word — a sense of solemnity, of being in some awesome place? Perhaps, for some people, particularly older people, but not for very many people today.

Do we think that religious language is necessary in order to convey religious truths? I wonder. In the first place, there are no "religious" truths, are there? There are only truths. If something is true, it is true, whether it is "religious" or not. In the second place, Jesus didn't seem to use religious language very much. He did when he was talking to religious people such as the priests, Pharisees, scribes. But even then he also tended to use nonreligious language such as "hypocrites," "whitewashed tombs." He used ordinary language — about flowers and birds and housewives and Samaritans. I doubt that he felt any particular need to use religious language.

Do we use religious language because we are afraid that if we do not, we will only be giving our own opinions, only talking about our own experiences — that we will not be preaching the word of God? But God has to speak in ordinary language, not a special language, does he not? He comes to us and at us through ordinary events. Is he confined to religious words? It is easy to escape from saying anything about God at all by using religious language. But suppose you really want to communicate (and this is often an unwarranted assumption). For example, suppose I say: "There is a group in this congregation that is mad at another group in this congregation. How about getting together and talking about what is bothering you?" That is ordinary language. But suppose I say, "God was in Christ reconciling the world to himself." That sounds safe enough, but very few people would know what I meant, and even fewer would ever apply it to the problem of two factions in the church who are fighting each other. Yet, I would say that God is at work now in this hostility among the people in the church and what he wants is for these groups to get together and "hash it out." It makes very little difference whether God was reconciling the world to himself in Christ or not if he isn't working now to bring people together. Right?

I am not concerned about giving examples in everyday life of what certain theological concepts mean. That is, I am not saying, "Now God's reconciliation in Christ is illustrated by two factions in a congregation speaking to each other." No, this is not what I mean. I do not think that our lives are "illustrations" of Biblical or theological truths. Our living is truth. What two groups in the congregation do together doesn't illustrate something. Rather, there is where truth is — the Jones faction is sitting down with the Smith faction and they are having it out. This is where it is happening. Call it reconciliation if you wish. You can say, "See — this is what Jesus was talking about." But it wasn't. Because Jesus was talking about events two thousand years ago — not now. You can say, "I think it is great that these two factions are getting together and now maybe we can get something done in this church." Now you're talking. That makes sense to me.

Suppose I say from the pulpit, "God loves you." There are people who may say to themselves, "Isn't that wonderful!" But what have I really communicated? Suppose I say: "I care about you. I care about you enough to share with you something that is bothering me. I am bothered by the fact that I haven't challenged you enough to use the talents you have in doing something worthwhile." That might communicate a bit better. I should mean it, however. I better start challenging you specifically and personally to use your unique talents in a particular way. Suppose I say this: "There are people in this church who care about you — we have decided to call a meeting of the parents of the senior high youth in this church, and we are going to talk about your common problems and see if we can do anything about the problems." Such a statement ought to begin some communication. If we actually follow through, then communication can amount to something. Isn't this kind of language more significant than saying, "God loves you"? I am reminded of an old joke: A girl is saying to her boyfriend, "You don't really love me and my hands are cold." The boy responds, "God loves you and you can sit on your hands." If the boy held her hand, she wouldn't care whether God loved her or not. Or, perhaps this is the way God can love her — through this boy.

Try preaching a sermon in ordinary language. No religious words. Just talk about what is happening. Talk about the significance of what is happening and not happening. There is good precedent for this. Jesus didn't talk much about love of neighbor. But he did talk about a Samaritan who cared about someone. Jesus cared about his disciples. He healed people. Jesus didn't talk much about God's forgiveness. He forgave.

Religion

If the minister is separated from the layman and does not known the layman's world — the fate of most ministers — then he is limited in what he can preach about. Usually the minister preaches about " religion." He preaches about religion because this is the only area of life that he and the layman have in common. And also because he, the minister, has become something of an expert on religion.

Some examples of religion-oriented sermons are sermons that deal with religious practices such as churchgoing, devotional life, and Christian education. Sermons on such topics are not sermons about normal everyday life, but are sermons about religion. They tell you how to live in that realm known as religion. Sermons about Christian doctrines are usually sermons about religion. Most people do not bother themselves daily about the meaning of the doctrine of the Trinity or about Christology or the inspiration (or lack of it) of the Bible. Sermons about morality are more often than not sermons about religion. They are about what is right and wrong — ideally. What are the religious rules? — that sort of thing. Not what do you do when the boss will fire you if you tell the truth. Many sermons that we hear today are about the nature of the church. They are usually about religion. Such sermons speak of the church as if it were an entity in itself that deserved to exist. What is the church? The church, so the preachers say, is proclaimer, teacher, servant, etc. But even the term " servant " usually refers to what the church as an organization can do to justify its existence. Its existence, that is, as a religious institution. To put it crudely, if the church cannot justify its existence by providing a place for preaching, worship, and teaching, then maybe it can still maintain itself if it gets somewhat involved in social issues. " Church and world " are discussed.

This usually means that we have to send church members into what is called the " public sector " and do in an amateur way what is already being done professionally by people whose living depends on it. To put it crudely again: Why should a Negro welcome me, a white churchgoer, to join him in his fight for recognition if the reason I am doing it is that I think I " should " as a church member? Doesn't he really need people who care about their own recognition and integrity and power as he does? Does he really need church types who are seeking to justify their own existences as church members?

Isn't it true that when we invite people to accept Christ as their Savior, we are really inviting them to get interested in religion? Following Jesus means finding out what religion is all about and then doing religious acts. Put more simply, it means serving on boards and committees, teaching in the church school, and singing in the choir. This is following Jesus? This is commitment to Christ? Isn't this really just " practicing religion "? It isn't a question of Who wants it?; it is a question of Who needs it?

Are we as preachers interested in having people become religious? We cry for commitment. Commitment to what? To maintain your interest in religion, religious ideas, religious problems, in order that we may preach to you. Since we preachers only know about religion, you people have to find out about it so that we can talk to you. You, you laymen — you prove to us that you are interested in religion and are willing to give some time to it, and then we will talk with you and we will absolve you of all your sins because now you are committed.

Jesus did not ask people to get interested in religion. In fact, he cautioned against such practices. Cautioned? Railed against them! There was too much religion in Israel as it was. Who needed more? Jesus called people to follow him. Not into the Temple, but onto the roads — healing, bringing people together, talking about what matters, visiting those whom no one else visited such as the poor, the rich, the outcast, the pariahs. Not in order to get people to be more religious, not in order to salve the consciences of the disciples, but because he wanted to go where the people were getting hurt and were seeing hope.

A person can become a minister and know a lot about religion and virtually nothing about ordinary living, about how people deal with each other, the crying of men and women and their laughing. I don't need religion. You don't need it. All we need is someone who cares about us, and something to do that is worthwhile, and God who makes it important forever. Don't preach to me about religion. Preach to me about being a human being and the pain of it and the joy of it and why God needs us and why we need him and each other and whether anything matters or not.

A Successful Sermon

How do you judge as to the success of a sermon? There are a number of possibilities. Let us look at a few:

1. A sermon is successful if the response that is called for is the response that is made by the congregation. For example, suppose that the sermon calls for action in the neighborhood. The action called for is a surveying of the needs of the neighborhood and a working out of ways to meet the needs. A successful sermon has been preached if the people, following the sermon, conducted the survey and began to meet the needs. Of course, this would require more than one sermon, wouldn't it? It would also mean that people needed to know how to take a survey. Prior to that, it would mean that people would have to be convinced that a survey was needed — that they

needed to find out what the needs are in the neighborhood. Indeed, a series of sermons would probably have to be preached before people would begin to see that such a survey was needed. More than sermons would be needed. Boards and committees, small groups in the congregation, and congregational meetings would have to deal with the neighborhood and the rationale for going into the neighborhood. The sermon in this case would be successful if the survey was made and the needs met. But a lot of other work would have to be done as well. This shows again that the sermon does not stand by itself. A " call to action " type of sermon must be preached within the context of a congregational concern which predates the sermon or which provides the context for the sermon. It is not just the sermon that is successful, but the whole thrust of the congregation's work.

2. A sermon is successful if it gets people to think about something in a new and fresh way. Let us say that a sermon deals with salvation. Salvation is thought of as an individual deciding to commit his life to Christ. But can a sermon bring this about? Perhaps a sermon can stimulate a desire on the part of a person for commitment. But a sermon is really only a part of this process. Something needs to be done in preparing people to receive such a call to commitment. Something also needs to be done in the way of following up on the commitment that is made. Commitment is not a once-and-for-all-time matter. Again, it is not the sermon in itself that needs to be successful. It is what happens in the wider context of the life of the church.

3. A sermon is successful if it illumines a passage of Scripture. Many think that this is important. This might be called a " learning success." Of course, the assumption is that the congregation wants to receive this kind of illumination. The Scripture is evidently in some sense authoritative for them.

This cannot be assumed as readily in our day as it used to be. It would seem to me that the passage of Scripture should be chosen very carefully for its universal appeal and application and for its relevancy to the particular preaching situation.

4. A sermon is successful if it sheds light on the meaning of a situation that is faced in common by the members of the congregation. Let us suppose that the preacher is shedding light on the situation the congregation faces in its attempt to minister to the youth of the community. He is illuminating the problem and is offering some possible solutions. Again, this assumes that the congregation cares about the youth in the community, that this is a felt need, a problem that " grabs " them. Or it means that they care potentially, that is, they care subconsciously but it takes a sermon to bring their caring up to the level of consciousness. Also the sermon will not really be successful unless there is some kind of follow-up — that is, unless some people start working on the problem.

Looked at objectively a sermon is usually successful only when there is preparation for it, and when it is followed up in some specific way. This is true of any speech. The listeners must care at least subconsciously about what the speaker is saying. The listeners then need to be given opportunities to respond to the call or challenge that was presented. Unless this happens the speech or sermon is really not much more than entertainment — perhaps mildly amusing, mildly enlightening (for the twenty minutes that it is being preached), but not transforming. We need to ask if we want sermons to be a part of the renewing of persons or not. If we do, then preparation and follow-up are essential.

Postscript:

The television news specials, which focus on a particular problem such as migrant workers, the war in Vietnam, racial tensions, have a twofold effect. First, they illumine a situation. They " educate." Second, they give the appearance of doing something significant — even of doing something on our behalf. In other words, if you or I see a program on racial tensions, we may say: " Yes, that is a real problem all right. Thank God some people are doing something about it." Or we may say: " Man, I don't see how those people live that way. It must really be rough." Or: " Well, that's only one side of the picture. All these news shows arc biased." No matter what our reaction, we know that we can turn off the set or wait until *Gunsmoke* comes on and we won't have to do anything specifically about racial tensions. We have been " educated." Perhaps we feel that we have dealt with the problem vicariously. We may even feel purged of our guilt. But we know that no one is going to jump out of the television set, come over to us and say, " Now how about joining the NAACP?" And yet, isn't this what needs to be done in a worship service, or as the follow-up to a worship service? We can hear a beautiful sermon about race relations, and it can have the same effect as a television news special. We know that neither the minister nor anyone else in the congregation is going to ask any of us to respond specifically to what was said. We can live vicariously through the sermon. The preacher dealt with the problem. We were there and we assume that therefore we have dealt with the problem. But we haven't. Can preachers afford to do religious entertaining anymore? Even prophetic religious entertaining?

Sensitizing

Let us imagine that I am telling you about my wife's caring for me — her ability to give of herself to me. Suppose I tell you of particular instances when this happened. I am giving you a slice of life. It means something to me. It is important to me and to her. Perhaps it is even significant to you if you can somehow identify or " connect " with my experience. But suppose I go a step farther. Suppose I say that in my wife's love for me, God is loving me. This is a theological statement. I am using religious language. What is the effect of using such language?

In my wife's loving me, God is loving me — that takes something away from what my wife is doing. It makes her God's tool. It is as if God is acting in disguise. When my wife is relating to me, I don't want God getting in the way. My wife has a right to love me without bringing God into it at all. There is a suggestion of something phony, something not quite kosher, about my wife's caring for me if I speak of it as God's loving of me.

In my wife's loving me, God is loving me. I suppose this means that my wife's loving of me is pretty important. It means that her loving of me is " rooted " in what is basic to the universe. Her loving is of ultimate, even eternal significance. Her loving is God's loving *for me*. I don't know. I really don't need eternal significance in order to respond to my wife's loving of me. There is something significant for me, eternal or not, that " gets to me " more than anything God might do. I care more about my wife and her caring for me than I care about whether it has ultimate or eternal significance or is rooted in the universe or not.

Perhaps if I shift from thinking about whether or not God is loving me through my wife. Perhaps if I concentrate on my relationship with my wife. Am I really receiving her caring, or do I push her away? Do I let her know how much I need her? Do I care enough about her to tell her how I feel about her, even when I am hostile to her? These may be much more important questions than the question of what God has to do with all of this.

Try this one on for size: It is in my acquaintance with the Bible and Christian thought, with people who have wrestled with the questions of life, in my knowing about Jesus, that I have become sensitized to such questions as those in the paragraph immediately preceding this one. It is the sensitizing that is important. Perhaps this is where God is at work most powerfully — in sensitizing me to ask questions that matter — in sensitizing me to feel what it is important to feel.

But what if my Christian upbringing had not helped to sensitize me to relationships with other people? A lot of so-called Christian upbringing has not done so. A lot of it didn't do so for me either. Sometimes Christian upbringing alienates us from other people — particularly if it emphasizes what makes " us " different.

Why don't we talk about human relationships? Why don't we help to sensitize people to the questions that need to be asked about our relationships, to the agonies that need to be experienced in such relationships, to the hurts and doubts and hates and loves that are a part of deeply felt living? In doing this let us talk about Jesus and about how he treated people. Let us talk about the religious traditions of men and of what they say about treating people. Let us set up situations where we can confront each other and speak to each other the caring words that we all need to hear.

Something to Take Home with You

" Give them something they can take home with them."

When a child is in kindergarten, he likes to take something home with him that he has done that day in school. Something to show Mommy and Daddy. Why? I suppose it is partly because then he thinks that he has accomplished something that day. Or maybe that is more the teacher's view.

("I don't want the parents to think that I am a complete dud, so I will give him something to show for his and my efforts.") He probably also likes to take something home to share his accomplishment or feeling of accomplishment with his parents, whose acceptance he needs. "See — look what I did in school today." "That is very good, Jackie. I am very proud of you. You are doing a lot better."

We often hear that sermons are supposed to give people something they can take home with them. Like what? A good feeling, perhaps. A feeling that life can be lived and that it is at least ultimately worthwhile. Or possibly a feeling of guilt. A feeling that I am not doing too good a job of living, and it is good for me to hear this because now I will do better. Now I am being taken seriously. A feeling. The preacher gives us a feeling and this feeling we take home and nourish and say to ourselves that we got something out of the sermon.

Sometimes we mean that we should get an idea or a "thought" out of the sermon. "By George, forgiving is rough for the one forgiven as well as for the forgiver. That was sure true when Maud forgave me for what I did a year ago." This particular thought is a psychological or, if you prefer, religious insight. It is a thought that gives us a way of looking at our lives that may be helpful.

The thought that we might get out of the sermon could be the illuminating of a Biblical text or a doctrine or a contemporary religious issue. Something to take home with us.

Back to the kindergartner. We could say, "It doesn't matter what he takes home, just so he takes something." But it does matter to the child. If he is concerned about accomplishing something, he wants to take home something that is really an accomplishment — something that was a challenge for him — something that he has done that was better than what he did before — something he can be proud of. He wants his parents to admire him for doing something that is worthy of admiration. This something must be something that is of worth. Haven't you known the experience of seeing your child bring home something that he knows is not well done, not up to his standard, and you admired it and he knew and you knew and he knew you knew that it wasn't really worth much?

I can bring a good feeling home from church. It may not be of much worth. I can feel uplifted, stirred, and happy. And after a couple of hours it wears off. I could probably have received the same feeling from a walk in the woods or a musical comedy or from playing with my kids. Why spend the time in church? Why pay the preacher to give me happy feelings?

There are feelings and there are feelings. I could be stirred to the depths of my emotions. The preacher may have told of ways in which people have dealt with severe emotional crises — the real ways, not the phony through-prayer-alone ways. And I am going through a crisis. I feel that if others can make it, I can make it. This is not just a happy feeling. It is a conviction and a hope. Suppose the preacher shows how this hope is at the heart of the gospel, the gospel of a man who came through in spite of a cross, and of disciples who made it in spite of their frailty. This goes a bit deeper than mere happy feelings. If this is what we mean by getting something out of a sermon — fine. But this something we get must be significant. It must touch us at a very deep level, or it is not worth it. No preacher is going to touch us at a deep level, unless he has been so touched, unless he has experienced the power of God to give men a hope that brings us through the crisis experiences of life.

Possibly I bring home a "thought." What kind of thought? "Oh, I see. When Jesus said to Peter, 'Get behind me, Satan!' he meant that Peter was tempting him to reveal himself as the

Messiah and this would be bad because it would mislead the Jews into thinking that they would be led against the Roman enemy. Isn't that interesting? I always wondered what that meant." Interesting? Perhaps. Significant? I wonder. So I learned something about a Biblical passage that I didn't know before. So what? Do I care? Do I care whether or not Jesus wanted to reveal himself as the Messiah to the Jews? Isn't that their problem? Or Jesus' problem? It isn't my problem. It is a " Bible gem." But we don't have time for Bible gems in an age when people are dying needlessly, races are crying for their freedom and manhood, and men and women all over the civilized world are living lives of " quiet desperation." Let us not waste our time by going to church to hear some " gems from the Bible."

Merely because something is in the Bible, that does not mean that it is significant for us. I know a man who believes that if he only reads enough of the Bible to his congregation on a Sunday morning something is bound to happen. After all, it is the " Word of God." This is bibliolatry. It is also a belief in the magic power of sacred words.

Turn again to the passage about Jesus, Peter, and Satan. Throughout the Gospels, we find instances of Jesus' wrestling with the problem of his self-identity. In this passage he asks Peter, " Who do you say that I am? " Peter answers that he is the Messiah. But Peter cannot tell Jesus who he is. No one can tell Jesus who he is. Peter can use the title " Messiah," but Peter does not know what the title means, he only knows Jesus. There is a distance between Jesus and his disciples, indeed, between Jesus and all men. Men are unable to tell Jesus who he is, to define his self-identity. This speaks to me in my own time. James Agee in *A Death in the Family* (p. 14; Avon Books, 1957) speaks of a boy's relatives and of what they can and cannot do for him:

Those receive me, who quietly treat me, as one familiar and well-beloved in that home: but will not, oh, will not, not now, not ever; but will not ever tell me who I am.

This is true of Jesus and it is true of all of us. Because of this, we take hope. No one can tell us who we are. Therefore, we must work it out through our own experiments with identity, our own testing and trying. Perhaps, like Jesus, we go to our destiny not knowing precisely who we are, but living as if we did and dying to our desire for certainty. This speaks to me. I cannot know if it speaks to you. I think it is worth considering. It is not one more " Bible gem."

" Give them something they can take home with them." But deliver us from insignificance, from trifles, from wasting our time in a time when time is precious, our greatest gift, our redemption from the void.

Epilogue

It may be helpful to make two comments before bringing this book to a close. The first comment is a confession. I have not striven for consistency in this book. The careful reader will note that there are many contradictions. One essay will contradict another. There are a number of reasons for this. I have tried to present a variety of points of view. I do not think that I have a direct line to God's thoughts, and I feel that truth will be revealed to us only if we look at various possibilities. Furthermore, I find that I often contradict myself, that I am inconsistent in my own views — even those which I hold to passionately. Perhaps this proves my humanity. It is certainly no argument for my divinity. I find that one view of preaching "grabs" me for a while, and then I make a turn to the left or right and begin preaching another view. I hope this is healthy. Perhaps you who are preachers find that you have similar experiences. Isn't life more a matter of testing various possibilities than it is of settling down to one straight line of thought or action?

The second comment has to do with my basic theological perspective. I am struck by a point made in the third chapter of Genesis. The serpent says to Eve: God knows that when you eat the fruit "your eyes will be opened, and you will be like God, knowing good and evil" (ch. 3:5). After the fall, God says, "Behold, the man has become like one of us, knowing good and evil" (v. 22). It seems to me that the basic temptation that man faces is the temptation to deny his humanity and become godlike. Religion is often used to help bring this about. Many believe that the goal of religion is to make people into godlike beings. But I believe that man must accept his status as man, and should receive his humanity as his greatest gift. To me this means that we human beings should resist the temptation to work for eternal security, infinite knowledge, success, identification with an image that is not who we are, and freedom from anxiety, failure, and death. When we strive to do something that will "set us up" for eternity, whether it be commitment to Christ or religiously-oriented self-flagellation, we are trying to be gods and not men. When we want to know precisely what is right and wrong, what we should do with our lives, and what we should think and feel, we are trying to be gods and not men. When we work doggedly for success in all realms, as if success were possible and we could know when we were succeeding, we are striving to be like a god. When we worship an image and try to mold ourselves according to this image, whether it is an image given to us by our society or our religion, we are worshiping a graven image and we are striving to be gods and not men. When we expect to achieve freedom from the pains of living and the fact of dying, we are trying to be serene and immortal — like gods in a heaven — but not like men on earth. We need to affirm our humanity, with its mortality, bondage, inadequacies, pain, and joy. Let God be God. Let men be men. May we combine our weeping over our lack of divinity with our rejoicing over our gift of humanity. Thank God we are human. Being God would be more than any of us could bear.